AMERICAN SOCIETY FOR INDUSTRIAL SECURITY
1625 PRINCE STREET
ALEXANDRIA, VA 22314
(703) 519-6200

Sticky Fingers

A CLOSE LOOK AT AMERICA'S

FASTEST-GROWING CRIME

Wm. W. McCullough

A DIVISION OF AMERICAN MANAGEMENT ASSOCIATIONS

Library of Congress Cataloging in Publication Data

McCullough, Wm. W.
  Sticky fingers.

  Includes bibliographical references.
  1. Embezzlement--United States. I. Title.
HV6679.M33   364.1'62   80-69696
ISBN 0-8144-5688-X   AACR2

© 1981 AMACOM
A division of American Management Associations, New York.

First Printing

This book is respectfully dedicated to the many thousands of trustworthy, devoted, and loyal bookkeepers, clerks, and other employees who are a part of the "preciously small minority."

PREFACE

Because of such frequent headlines as BANKER BOLTS TO BERMUDA WITH BONDS AND BLONDE, the average respectable citizen tends to regard the crime of embezzlement as an activity confined primarily to the upper echelons of financial and corporate personnel. Exposed to the lurid details of such debacles as Equity Funding and Home-Stake (and the piddling penalties imposed on those guilty), it is understandable why Mr. Average Respectable Citizen holds a strong conviction that most of those who deal in high finance and corporate affairs are crooks, period. Concurrently, our friend also believes sincerely that, except as noted above, most people are honest and trustworthy, striving to adhere faithfully to the precepts of the Ten Commandments and the Boy Scout Oath.

Wrong—on both counts!

The *daily* pilfering by employees from the cash and stock of America's millions of small and medium-size businesses, stores, and offices far exceeds such losses among *Fortune*'s 500 in a week or maybe a month. Secondly, most people are *not* honest. Reams of statistics from bonding companies and security agencies irrefutably disclose that the majority of people will steal if they get a chance, another sizable segment will steal if they think they can get away with it, and only a preciously small minority will not steal under any circumstances.

The purpose of this book is to take a close look at the crime of embezzlement or employee fraud, to study those who do it and how they do it, and to make a few observations and suggestions for the protection of those who trust their money and merchandise to employees, all with the hope that some of its readers may profit from its contents.

A fatherly word of caution to those who may be attracted to this volume as a possible do-it-yourself handbook for aspiring embezzlers—forget it! All of the cases cited herein are the sad stories of people who thought they were smarter than they were, who thought they had discovered a Mother Lode that could be mined forever, and who thought that they would never get caught. If only they had known that the perfect embezzlement has never been perpetrated, and never will be, and that even the smallest defalcation leaves a trail like a moose through a snowbank, clearly visible to a skilled and patient investigator.

Yes, growing earthworms might be more profitable. It is certainly safer.

I am not a psychologist, a sociologist, or a criminologist. I do not claim to be an expert on the subject of embezzlement. I am only a public accountant who has spent more than 40 years ministering to the fiscal health of hundreds of small and medium-size business and professional clients. In that span of time, inevitably, it has been my unpleasant duty to pull out by the heels a goodly corps of culprits, male and female, who could not distinguish between thine and mine.

PREFACE

From those experiences, and from a lifelong professional interest in the phenomenon of human cupidity, have evolved the opinions, observations, and practical advice herein set forth. It is hoped that the sharing of these thoughts may directly benefit some of the millions of small and medium-size employers who are the present and potential victims of employee dishonesty. Attorneys, security officers, insurance agents, and fellow accountants, all constantly aware of the imminence and incidence of embezzlement, may also glean a few bits of information useful in their never-ending efforts to thwart the designs of the greedy.

And, finally, if the reading of this book brings one tempted individual to a sober realization of the futility and stupidity of defalcation—and the merits of trustworthiness—it will have served its purpose well.

Wm. W. McCullough

ACKNOWLEDGMENTS

Few successful dissertations on serious subjects can be written without the aid of outside resources and the generous assistance of persons more skilled in specialized fields than the author professes to be. I have been a most fortunate recipient of the contributions of others, and no formal acknowledgment can adequately express my gratitude and appreciation.

It was Donald R. Cressey, Professor of Sociology, University of California, Santa Barbara, and author of the first definitive treatise on the psychology of embezzlement, who provided the initial encouragement to attempt the writing of this volume. His sustained interest throughout the project and his critical review of the finished manuscript were material contributions toward completion.

Dean N. Ray, Professor of Criminology, California State University, Fresno, also was most generous in his continued encouragement and constructive criticism.

Kenneth G. Hance, retired Professor of Speech, Michigan State University, author of textbooks and former president of the Speech Association of America,

ACKNOWLEDGMENTS

provided invaluable suggestions on organization and syntax, and reviewed in detail the finished work.

Phillip S. Cronin, Assistant United States Attorney, Eastern District of California, and George L. Thurlow, Juvenile Court Referee, County of Tulare (California), constructively criticized the manuscript and approved it for legal accuracy.

Guy S. Balser, Vice President of the California State Board of Accountancy and past president of the National Society of Public Accountants, reviewed the manuscript and concurred in the accounting conclusions reached therein.

Robert C. Parremore, Assistant Manager, Fidelity Department, Surety Association of America; Joseph P. Keyes, Vice President, Public Relations, American Management Associations; Gordon L. Williams, Vice President, Operations Division, National Retail Merchants Association; Donald E. Vaile, Assistant Vice President, Fidelity–Surety Department, United States Fidelity and Guaranty Company; and Francis J. McCullough, Vice President, Valley Distributing Company, a division of Lucky Stores, Inc., all supplied valuable statistical information, offered pertinent suggestions, and reviewed the finished manuscript.

To each of these good people, heartfelt thanks are extended.

CONTENTS

PART III   The Defensive Posture

Part I

THE ANATOMY
OF THE CRIME

1

TAKE A NUMBER

That a crime so entrenched and flourishing as embezzlement, and as old as the human race, could generate so little solid statistical information on its frequency and cost is almost unbelievable. Any serious effort to gather and consolidate hard numerical facts from scattered and often conflicting sources soon bogs down in a morass of estimates, "guesstimates," conjectures, and hunches. If the investigator is a professional accountant, accustomed to dealing in precision and exactitude, the experience can be frustrating, to say the least.

5

Whereas students of violent crime—murder, robbery, rape—have at their instant disposal volume upon volume of documented data from informative sources ranging from the local constable to the FBI, researchers of so-called white-collar crime, which includes embezzlement, must make do with tentative and sketchy estimates supplied by bonding companies, security agencies, and trade associations. Since only a small minority of all employees are bonded, since security agencies are engaged primarily by larger employers, and since usually only the big national and regional firms respond to the questionnaires of national trade associations, it is obvious that information from these sources is, at best, only a fragmentary—but frightening—indication of the magnitude of the total problem. It is the logical projection of this limited and nonrepresentative sample down into the vast area occupied by the nation's small and medium-size enterprises that supports a basic contention of this treatise, to wit: that the *recorded* losses from embezzlement and employee fraud are mere chicken feed compared with the *unrecorded* losses sustained, for the most part, by smaller concerns.

Does anyone want to argue?

Funded by a grant from the Law Enforcement Assistance Administration of the Department of Justice, the American Management Associations (AMA) completed in 1977 a comprehensive study of nonviolent crimes against business.[1] Of a grand total of "best judgment" estimates amounting to $30 billion to $40 billion of annual losses for crimes ranging from shoplifting to credit card fraud, employee dishonesty topped the list at a possible $14 billion, with embezzlement of cash set at $4 billion and pilferage of tools and merchandise at

$5 billion to $10 billion. To this summary, the report adds this sobering afterthought: *". . . perhaps much more."* (Italics added)

Who pays for these losses?

The AMA report estimates conservatively that 15 percent of the retail price of merchandise is meant to cover the cost of nonviolent crimes, of which employee dishonesty is the major portion. It is to the customer that the loss surely must be passed on if the merchant is to stay in business. Unfortunately, not everyone in business is alert enough to shift the burden before the blow falls, for the report also suggests that 20 percent of firms that go out of business each year do so because of employee crimes against them. A major bonding company, United States Fidelity and Guaranty Company, states that 30 percent of all business bankruptcies can be blamed on employee dishonesty.[2]

On the basis of information gathered from its members in 1976, the National Retail Merchants Association (NRMA) believes that inventory shortage alone exceeds 2 percent of retail sales and that employee theft, not shoplifting as had been expected, is the major cause.[3] Sixty large department and specialty stores, with annual sales ranging from $10 million to $1 billion, supplied the data. Since it can be assumed that these stores suffer losses of that magnitude in spite of the most effective security and inventory control systems that can be devised, where does that leave the majority of smaller merchants who go on blissfully, year after year, believing that their employees are honest and that protective measures are too expensive or are an unnecessary nuisance? Further, the NRMA says, "The impact of losses from crime in relation to the size of the firm, as measured by its receipts, indicates that small business suffers an impact from crime which is 3.2 *times* that of firms with receipts of over $5 million."

Most of the cited statistics arise in the area of retail merchandising, but embezzlement is not an activity confined to retail trade. Every business larger than a one-man peanut stand offers plundering possibilities to the employee who is looking for them. Contractors of all kinds can be stolen blind of tools and materials. Banks and other financial institutions, whose merchandise is money, are particularly vulnerable. Doctors, lawyers, accountants, and even farmers have felt the sting of thieving employees. It would seem that a mom and pop enterprise would be practically immune, but not infrequently divorce proceedings disclose otherwise.

There was a time when fire was the major loss sustained by business, but it has now lost its preeminence. According to the United States Fidelity and Guaranty Company, "The losses to employers from embezzlement exceed those caused by fire in a substantial measure."[2] Again one must wonder how a criminal loss of such magnitude could fail to produce meaningful statistics, or even a general public awareness of its pervading existence. It has got to be the best-kept secret in the annals of crime.

There is a dramatic contrast between fire and embezzlement. Fire is like the sudden trauma of a severe accident, plainly visible to its victim and to the public, spectacular and dramatic. Its damage generally is reparable or replaceable, its consequences usually not fatal to the business. Embezzlement, on the other hand, is like a silent, insidious cancer, hidden and unsuspected, gnawing at the vitals and sapping the lifeblood. When finally discovered, its effects may be irreversible and its damage irreparable. A terminal case, the business may die "after a lingering illness."

Farfetched? Ask any embezzlement victim.

With some admitted literary license, this book has been subtitled "a close look at embezzlement, America's fastest-growing crime." Though the assumption is not susceptible to documentary proof, there is ample evidence that it is not far from its mark. National Retail Merchants Association reports that crime against retailers increased 46 percent between 1971 and 1975,[3] and American Management Associations places at 10 percent the current annual growth rate.[1] (Employee dishonesty, as previously noted, is the major portion of the general category of crime against business.) As early as 1970, United States Fidelity and Guaranty Company stated flatly that embezzlement was "increasing at the rate of 15 percent each year,"[2] and statistics recently released by the Justice Department's Law Enforcement Assistance Administration indicate that, between 1974 and 1978, retail crime losses increased 72 percent and employee theft now constitutes 65 percent of the total—over three times the loss from shoplifting.[4]

With soaring expenses, shrinking margins of profit, and ever-increasing competition, the head of a small business is hard pressed to keep his doors open and remain solvent. Even his very survival is a subject of concern and conjecture among economists, financiers, and accountants. He is certainly in no position to share his hard-earned profits with thieving employees, and the delicate balance between financial solidity and insolvency may well hinge on his ability to plug the leaks. He can no longer afford to take a complacent "it-can't-happen-to-me" attitude or continue to play Russian roulette against the odds so overwhelmingly stacked against him.

In the closing paragraph of its study findings,[1] AMA states: "Small and medium-size businesses do not have effective security systems, and their executives are naive about the measures they can take to reduce crimes against them. They do not realize that loss prevention/ asset protection is just another management problem, amenable to solution by the application of standard management principles."

Let's have an instant replay on that—in slow motion:

1. Small and medium-size businesses do *not* have *effective* security systems.
2. Their executives are *naive* about the measures *they* can take to *reduce* crimes against them.
3. They do not realize that loss prevention/asset protection is *just another management problem, amenable to solution* by the application of *standard management principles.*

It can be done. It *must* be done. The situation is far from hopeless.

NOTES
1. *Crimes Against Business Project; Background, Findings, and Recommendations* (AMACOM, 1977).
2. *Forty Thieves* (Baltimore: United States Fidelity and Guaranty Company, 1970).
3. *Crime Against General Merchandise, Department and Specialty Stores* (New York: National Retail Merchants Association, 1977).
4. "Devising New Ploys to Outfox Thieves," *Chain Store Age Executive* (August 1979), pp. 160–164.

2

ALL SIZES
AND SHAPES

Embezzlers, like other people, come in all sizes and shapes, and in both sexes. There is no such thing as a typical embezzler, yet common characteristics are so often found that their frequency seems more than coincidental. Popular opinion notwithstanding, the mousey little wage slave who steals in desperation to feed his starving children or dying wife is rarely found among those who diddle with other people's money. Somehow, the Bob Cratchits of our society have a way of staying alive and solvent without the sacrifice of their integrity.

Quite to the contrary, embezzlers most often are

personable, outgoing, sociable people, the kind who get along nicely with fellow employees and are well regarded by their superiors. As a result they are usually receiving a good wage and may be under consideration for advancement. Their positions of trust have been earned fairly by proven performance, possibly over a long period. Their education generally has been above average; but even if not, they possess good intelligence and mental capacity.

Their other shortcomings and vices are few, or well concealed. Often they are active in such community affairs as Little League, Sunday school, PTA, or Girl Scouts, and they may be the first to volunteer to work on the company picnic or Christmas party or to play on the bowling team. On or off the job they display congeniality, sincerity, and self-confidence. In general they are people you would like to have in your home for dinner and an evening of bridge or as companions on a fishing trip.

And there may be a very good reason why they act like that—such esteem creates the indispensable guise behind which they can plan and commit their scheme of thievery. ("Good old Joe? Why, he would never steal a dime!") In many cases there is substantial evidence that the creation of a phony respectable image is a deliberate and consuming objective, a fact that explains why some apparently dedicated church trustees or seemingly devoted scoutmasters will occasionally make unpleasant headlines.

Scheming and crafty persons, appearances notwithstanding, are frequently antisocial loners, avoiding normal social contacts whenever possible. Driven by an insatiable greed, they can and do camouflage their true nature. Once apprehended, such persons often release a spectacular outburst of spite and malice, blaming everyone but themselves for their predicament.

By and large, most crimes are the sins of youth, decreasing in frequency as maturity develops with age. Not so with embezzlement. Here the lifetime annual incidence seems to increase progressively until middle age and then winds down slowly into the "golden years." There are good reasons for this profile.

First, the confidence and credence requisite for reaching a position of trust are not bestowed lightly upon youth. A good reputation must be earned, and that may take a few years.

Second, the possibilities for dipping into the till may not become apparent until after months or years of dealing with the routine fiscal procedures of the job. Some new plan of operation may have an overlooked loophole in it, or a change in personnel may have left some base uncovered, then suddenly the light dawns and the road to riches seems here and now.

Third, except when plans for larceny are premeditated, it may take years for a person to develop enough greed, or to perceive enough need, to overcome his scruples and take the plunge.

Finally, once a seemingly successful scheme of defalcation has been devised and implemented, and if the culprit is possessed of sufficient self-restraint, the process may go on for years before its inevitable discovery.

While there is no such thing as a typical embezzler, there is definitely a typical pattern of embezzlement. Almost invariably, the first dip into the till is of minor consequence—a few dollars or an inexpensive article. If discovery occurs, an honest mistake can be claimed, or, if that gambit does not wash, contrite admission and solemn promises of future rectitude may still get the rascal off the hook with nothing more than a reprimand.

Assuming no discovery, now follows the waiting

period, which may be a few days or a few weeks. Only time will tell whether the first venture was successful. When possibility of detection has become sufficiently remote, the neophyte embezzler must consider his options: He can try it again or he can forget it. Any decision at this time to go for another round will be clear, cold, and calculated. The second try will probably duplicate the first, including the waiting period and the gee-whiz routine if detected. Once titillated by the thrill of success, and with all moral prohibitions effectively quashed, the offender cannot control the welling greed that possesses him, and his thefts will steadily increase in frequency and amount until the certain day when his dreams of wealth crash down around him.

It is the predictability of this pattern that causes auditors to view with suspicion even the most trifling irregularity in generally accepted procedures for accounting for money or merchandise. It is their keen awareness of the gestative process of embezzlement that keeps them constantly on the alert for the first indication that controls have been breached. In view of this special knowledge, training, and experience, perhaps they can be pardoned for suspecting a worm in every apple.

For many embezzlers the burden of their guilt becomes at times almost unbearable. Being the hail-fellow-well-met type of person that they usually are, they are painfully aware of the ego-shattering consequences should their crime become known and their true nature revealed to their family and friends. Even the fear of punishment does not surpass in intensity the fear of loss of face.

With this load on their conscience, it is not surprising that a large number of trust violators break down and confess readily when first confronted with hard evidence of their wrongdoing. Voluntary disclosure, even before there is any suspicion, is also not unusual. Often these confessions gush out like the rupture of a water-filled balloon, and this purging may be followed by expressions of relief that the grand charade has played its last act and the great burden has been lifted.

Not all confessors, however, are so naive. Some confessions will be limited to those sums and acts of which the culprit believes the investigator is already aware. Grudging, piecemeal additional admissions will follow only as new evidence is presented, and each addition will be sworn to be "all that there is." This cat-and-mouse game usually can be quickly terminated by accusing the suspect of a total sum far in excess of that suspicioned. The shock of this charge will call forth an instant and vigorous denial, probably followed by the blurting out of a smaller figure that ultimately may be determined to be surprisingly accurate.

A frequently noted element in cases that have long gone undetected, and particularly in those in which the miscreant has greatly accelerated the frequency and amounts of his pilferings, is that he seems to have thrown all caution to the winds and abandoned all effort at concealment. It is as though he has been seized with sudden stupidity, supreme overconfidence, or perhaps even some kind of "death wish" to be apprehended and get it over with.

The amazing conceit displayed by many embezzlers faced with arrest and prosecution is unbelievable. Vociferously, they protest that they have done nothing dishonest, that they are not criminals, and that they resent being thrown in the pokey along with common thieves, rapists, and muggers. They struggle valiantly to the bitter end to preserve the tattered remnants of their ego and respectability.

However, when the chips are down, and the penitentiary gate slams behind them, they usually become docile and cooperative prisoners. Their above-average intelligence and prior business experience may lead to the more desirable prison work assignments, and even to minor privileges. Generally, they do not have to associate intimately with the hardened criminals, have ample time for reflection and contemplation on the error of their ways, and come out of the penal experience with a new set of smarts more useful than the one that got them into trouble. The low incidence of recidivism among punished and presumably rehabilitated embezzlers is not, however, entirely due to the beneficial effects of incarceration. As the released offender quickly learns, positions of trust will be hard to come by for a long time, and what ego he has left will take a further beating as he is forced to accept jobs far below his mental capacity and skills level. His punishment did not end with his parole.

Because they are usually "such nice people," embezzlers frequently receive a misplaced sympathy from those who do not or cannot conceive the enormity of their crimes. Relatives and close friends in particular can become rabidly defensive and sometimes abusive to the point that the victim almost becomes the villain. Law enforcement officials, juries, and judges tend to treat crimes of trust violation lightly. Their rationale seems to be that, because the defendant had a clear record, no violence was displayed, and no one was physically damaged by his acts, the very dimensions of the crime have shrunk and its significance has diminished.

Notwithstanding such public sentiments, and their own distorted opinions of their honesty, embezzlers are essentially and irrefutably thieves. Moreover, they are thieves of the most despicable stripe, for their thievery has been based on the violation of that most sacred human relationship, the trust and confidence of one person in another. Cloaked in a guise of false respectability and held on a pedestal of trust by their unsuspecting victims, they have stolen deliberately, maliciously, and without mercy.

Compared with the embezzler, the gun-toting stick-up man is a gentleman and a scholar. *His* victim is *never* under any illusion as to the purpose of their encounter!

3

WHY DID
THEY STEAL?

In any investigation of criminal violation of financial trust, the question invariably arises, "Why did he (or she) do it?" Here we have a highly regarded person of average or better intelligence, with promise for the future of steady employment and reasonably good income, yet he has breached his trust, destroyed his good name, and blighted the rest of his life. Why? Finding the answer to that question becomes almost as impelling as determining the amount of the defalcation.

A simplistic answer, of course, would be that he thought he needed the money, but the speculation cannot be dismissed so easily. Further information might reveal one or more of such seeming causes as living beyond his means, too much liquor, gambling, playing the stock market, another woman, or heavy debts. But these are not reasons—they merely indicate the disposition of the pilfered funds. Even though the offender himself uses such generalizations to explain or excuse his filchings, they all beg the question, and the basic query remains unanswered.

An eminent sociologist, Donald R. Cressey, in the first definitive study of embezzlement and its causes, has advanced a persuasive theory concerning the fundamental cause for criminal violation of financial trust:

> Trusted persons become trust violators when they conceive of themselves as having a financial problem which is nonshareable, are aware that this problem can be secretly resolved by violation of the position of financial trust, and are able to apply to their own conduct in that situation verbalizations which enable them to adjust their conceptions of themselves as trusted persons with their conceptions of themselves as users of the trusted funds or property.[1]

It is doubtful if many embezzlers would identify themselves with this postulation, but in their own words they might recite the gist of it with amazing accuracy, such as: "I was in a real jam that I couldn't tell anybody about; I thought I saw a way to get some money that would get me out of it without anybody knowing, so I took it. After all, I didn't intend to *steal*—I was just *borrowing*, as I truly intended to pay back every cent!"

Nonshareable situations seldom mushroom up over

night. At their inception they are generally the routine small problems with which most people have no difficulty in coping. But they can and do grow until they become an unbearable burden. The fact that their roots sometimes may lie in some human frailty of which the bearer is not very proud only compounds the pressure and aids in rendering the problem nonshareable, at least in the mind of its possessor.

The bright young executive with a nagging and extravagant wife or the faithful bookkeeper with a ne'er-do-well lush of a husband can easily drift into an extramarital affair, for example, which renders a formerly manageable situation totally unmanageable and a shareable problem totally nonshareable. Seldom can a normal human problem be solved by such a lapse. The person in an unbearable situation who seeks solace and solution from the bottle or in the arms of a lover winds up with *two* unbearable problems. Nor can gambling, on the horses or on the stock market, be regarded as a reliable source of funds. Recognition of these verities often comes too late. (Old Pennsylvania Dutch proverb: "Ach! Dot old ve should so soon become und smart so late!")

The nonshareable financial problem sometimes involves no moral dilemma. The employee who perceives himself as being unappreciated and/or underpaid, or who may have been subjected to unfair criticism, may not have the ability or courage to face up to his boss and talk out the problem frankly. As a result he stews in his own juice, his lips tight and his temperature rising until the flashpoint is reached. He is ready for a grab at the brass ring.

This lack of fortitude to come to grips with a problem while it is still at the shareable stage is not an exclusive shortcoming of embezzlers. Much of human mental anguish could be avoided or alleviated by early forthright action, including sharing the problem and seeking outside advice. The young executive could have secured a loan, perhaps from his employer, cleaned up his bills, and taken charge of the family finances. The bookkeeper could have stopped providing funds for the purchase of booze, and the unappreciated party could have had it out with the boss or sought another job. It is always easy to see what the *other* fellow should have done. We should trade problems with each other—then all would have perfect solutions.

The fundamental issue is not whether the financial problem actually was shareable or nonshareable. The point is that the one with the problem has come to the certain conclusion that it is nonshareable and that it does not have an honorable solution. The stage is now set for the next act.

Every person placed in a position of financial trust soon becomes thoroughly familiar with all the conditions and restrictions with which he is surrounded. If there is a breach or crack in the fiduciary wall, it will soon be noted. From that time on, only the conscience of the trustee stands between security and jeopardy of the trust property, and that barrier may be flimsy indeed.

It would be most naive to expect that one possessed with the knowledge of such a weakness could refrain from speculating on the opportunity for personal gain from exploiting the situation. Only superhuman rectitude could completely banish such thoughts. Not only will the plundering potential be assessed but also the practical means of concealment considered and the odds against discovery weighed. As long as these conjectures do not rise above the daydreaming level, no harm has been done; the cash is intact and the fidelity unviolated. The trouble arises with the intrusion of the nonshareable financial problem and the subsequent evolution of a frivolous daydream into a seriously considered scheme of defalcation.

One barricade remains to protect the corpus of the trust, and that is the ego of the potential embezzler. If he has a normal, healthy ego, he considers himself to be an honest and trustworthy person, and he recognizes that his associates share the same opinion. Now, he is faced with a decision that could lead to the destruction of that image, in his own mind and in the minds of others. He is not prepared to think of himself as a criminal, and he is aware of the possible penalties. If only he could find some justification for what he is planning to do—so the mental wheels begin to turn.

"I'm really not a crook, and I don't want to *steal* the boss's money," he rationalizes. "I'll just *borrow* it for a little while; and as soon as I get back on my feet, I will pay it all back."

Wonderful! The idea fits comfortably. His ego is undamaged—well, almost—his reputation unblemished—after all, no one will ever know—and the unshareable problem apparently solved.

The employee nursing the obsession that he is unappreciated and underpaid solves his moral dilemma with the decision that he will purloin just enough to bring his salary up to what it should be if his abilities were properly recognized and he were paid accordingly. Those rankling under the failure of the employer to make good on a promised salary raise, or to follow through on some casually mentioned possibility of a partnership interest, can justify their unilateral decision to share the wealth—after all, they are taking only what they would have had coming to them. The trouble is that all of these firm resolves to limit the withdrawals to a self-perceived actual need usually fall by the wayside. The vast majority of trust violators, flushed by the success of their first experimental peculations, are stricken with a "gold fever" that cannot be satiated, and they plunge deeper and deeper into the mire until the inescapable call comes, "Mrs. Jones, will you please come into my office?"

We have now thoroughly explored the proposition that people violate financial trust when:

1. They think they have an unshareable financial problem.
2. They see a possible solution through embezzlement.
3. They wrestle with their conscience, and conscience loses.

Everything seems to fit nicely into place—almost.

Now and then a culprit appears on the scene who does not seem to conform to some part of this general pattern, for instance, when there is no, or at least a minimal, apparent nonshareable financial problem. Perhaps such persons have a low threshold of financial pain, or maybe they have daydreamed too much about the loophole they discovered in the office procedures. Perhaps, like mountain climbers, they did it "because it was there," or maybe they simply have enjoyed the thrill, and the feeling of superior intellect, of putting something over on someone else. In such instances there is also considerable doubt about just how great a struggle it was to "adjust their conceptions of themselves as trusted persons with their conceptions of themselves as users of the entrusted funds or property."

Then there is the absconder who grabs and runs. He, too, must have a low threshold of financial pain and also much less difficulty in rationalizing. Whereas the average defalcator makes *some* effort to conceal his crime, the absconder says, "To hell with it," and takes off for parts he hopes will remain unknown.

Just as other human activity patterns change from time to time, there is evidence of recent change in the motivation and attitudes of embezzlers. One security agency reports

> ... theft higher than "normal" now. Detected employees generally show little remorse. Many state, "Everybody does it, so why pick on me?" Other attitudes indicate they do not feel [the crime] is serious, or they did it for an imagined wrong: "I worked 15 minutes overtime last week and I wasn't paid for it." For some time now, [we] have not run into a single detected thief who actually needed the money.[2]

Interesting, indeed!

In reading literature on embezzlement and other white-collar crimes, one often comes upon articles on, or references to, the theme "Why do honest people steal?" *They're putting us on!* "Why does water run uphill?" or "Why does the sun set in the east?" would be just as logical as theorems for debate and speculation. It could well be that this kind of fuzzy thinking is the very genesis of the popular attitudes that have permitted the dramatic rise in white-collar crime and that tolerate its continued existence.

Honesty is an absolute. There are no degrees or modifiers. A person cannot be *generally* honest, *usually* honest, or *sometimes* honest. Either he is honest under all conditions, circumstances, and pressures, or he is *dishonest*.

NOTES
1. Donald R. Cressey, *Other People's Money; A Study of the Social Psychology of Embezzlement* (Glencoe, Ill.: The Free Press, 1953).
2. Howard W. Hament, Director, Merit Protective Service, Inc., San Francisco. Personal communication, September 7, 1979.

4

THE FERTILE SOIL

Virtually every embezzlement has as its fertile soil
some negligence, carelessness, or ignorance on the
part of the employer, whether the employer is a
multimillion-dollar corporation or a crossroads merchant.
The shortcomings of the employer can range from plain
stupidity to contributory gross negligence or may be
simply a blind confidence that "it can't happen to me."
Essentially, it is the failure of the employer to establish
and preserve a sound working relationship with the
employee that creates the conditions in which the
dishonest person can function.

The first weakening of a sound working relationship may occur even before the employee is hired if the hiring process is faulty. All too many employers have an exaggerated opinion of their abilities as practical psychologists and judges of human nature. Regardless of a probable history of failure in picking winners, they persist in believing that their judgment is infallible. As a result, new employees go on the payroll with little, if any, investigation of their prior records of education and employment, checking of references, or inquiry into family relationships or general background. Some unpleasant surprises have resulted from such negligence.

Few small and medium-size businesses have a documented personnel policy or even the sketchiest written specifications for job performance. Such important matters as vacations, sick leave, health and hospital benefits, and overtime pay are dealt with on a hit-or-miss, case-by-case basis. The new employee may be turned over to a supervisor or another employee, who tells the newcomer what he *thinks* the rules and requirements are at the moment. Even that may change tomorrow if the boss decides to issue a new pronouncement, which often must filter down by word of mouth through the organization. No wonder the recruit may come to feel that he has joined up with a sloppy outfit.

Some employers regrettably still cling to the ancient attitudes of a strict master and servant relationship. It seems to have escaped their attention that those days are gone forever and that employees are human beings with moral, legal, and civil rights that can be ignored by the employer only at his own risk and peril. Fortunately, most employers have gotten the message. Cordial employment relationships do not require a palsy-walsy, first-name intimacy or a company picnic on the third Saturday of every month. In fact, there are indications that the extreme informality in personnel matters often practiced in modern business may be counterproductive. The average employee will settle for fair treatment, including adequate compensation, an occasional pat on the back for good work done, and, above all, free and open communication between management and staff. When these conditions exist, it is hard for resentment and grudges to build up, undermine morale, and create an environment in which self-perceived justifications for thievery exist.

No one expects employers to be paragons of virtue. They have the same moral strengths and weaknesses that their employees have, and the company grapevine will assure that employee awareness of any frailty will be widely disseminated. Statistically, there is growing evidence that industries and organizations noted for management-level, white-collar crime—tax evasion, payoffs, kickbacks, bribery, regulatory violations—also experience a higher-than-average rate of embezzlement and employee fraud. (Why not? "If the top brass is ripping off, why can't we peons do the same?") Thus larceny becomes a substitute for loyalty.

The employer, inescapably, is the creator of the moral tone of his organization. His responsibility cannot be abdicated; if he thinks for a moment that he can expect from his employees a higher degree of integrity than he practices, he is not only a crook but a fool.

The automobile dealer who instructs his mechanics to pad their time charges, the merchant who short-measures his merchandise, and the contractor who substitutes inferior materials have no squawk coming when they discover—as they certainly will—that they have been shafted by a dishonest employee. Nor should the doctor who regularly pockets cash fees from patients without recording them be shocked when he finds his receptionist doing the same thing.

That, Doctor, is called the monkey-see-monkey-do syndrome!

"Don't Fence Me In" is more than just a plaintive cowboy ballad. It is the instinctive human reaction to any form of restraint. Over the millennia, however, the race has learned that certain restraints are necessary if civilization is to be achieved. To confine human conduct to acceptable limits is the sole objective of law and order, social custom, and religious precept. The alternatives are anarchy, social disorder, and moral decay. Accordingly, we have learned to live with rules and regulations, and we tend to become very frustrated and uncomfortable when for any reason we are denied their firm guidance. We cannot function effectively unless we know what is expected of us.

If any business organization is to progress and prosper, it must set down and adopt the rules under which it expects to operate in order that all persons within the firm may understand them and work harmoniously and efficiently under them. Failure to do so is an invitation to bankruptcy. Every large business concern issues many volumes of policy and operating procedures that govern its every activity. On a reduced scale, proportionate to its size, a smaller business should do no less. Of the essential minimums, none are more important than the internal controls that cover the firm's fiscal affairs. Internal controls are simply a system of mandatory business procedures designed to protect the assets of the enterprise and assure the accuracy of its accounting records. Though the necessity for internal controls has been advocated for many years, some people in business still think that the term has something to do with thermostats.

The first premise of any system of internal controls is that responsibility for critical financial procedures will be divided between two or more persons, the more the better. Such ideal division of responsibility is generally impossible in a small organization, but many sound and fundamental procedures still can be put into effect. For instance, all voided checks should be carefully and permanently preserved, likewise all voided invoices and other serially numbered forms. Bank statements and cancelled checks should be received, opened, and reviewed by the owner or manager himself before being touched by any employee. Nonexistence or breach of these two basic procedures is the genesis of many defalcations. These and numerous other simple but effective steps can be taken, which will provide substantial protection to the business assets. The firm's independent public accountant is the proper person to study the existing practices employed in the handling of money and merchandise and to suggest practical improvements for greater security.

Few business firms today elect to go it alone without some assistance from an independent public accountant, either a P.A. or a C.P.A., and those firms that attempt to follow the do-it-yourself route in regard to their accounting and tax matters for the sake of economy often find that they have made a costly choice. True, accountants, like other skilled professionals, expect to receive fees proportionate to their worth and fully recognize that the real value of their services may not be immediately visible. As "business doctors," they provide services that are primarily preventive rather than corrective. When a business is in good health and prospering, the proprietor may be tempted to cut down on outside accounting services ("Why go to the doctor when you are feeling well?"). However, let him get socked with a husky income tax deficiency due to some technical boo-boo, or find that his bookkeeper has looted the bank account, and he soon realizes that his losses would have paid generous accounting fees for many months. Large business appreciates the worth and necessity of outside accounting assistance and so avoids the pitfalls and losses suffered more frequently by the smaller, unassisted concern that can ill afford the blow. Underutilization of accounting and other professionals is one of today's classic business mistakes.

The average businessman starting a new establishment would not dream of opening his doors until his every asset was literally plastered with fire insurance. The familiar sound of sirens, the flash of red fire wagons, and the black smoke pouring from some unfortunate premises keep the possibility of a similar loss to himself constantly in his mind. He just cannot afford to take a chance. Yet, this same "prudent" proprietor will go on for years, operating an enterprise that may have revenues in the hundreds of thousands or even millions annually, and with always a substantial portion of that amount invested in inventory, without a fidelity bond on a single employee. Let his insurance agent tell him that, according to statistics, 50 percent or more of his employees will steal from him if they get a chance, and he accuses the agent of using scare tactics to sell him unnecessary insurance. He's not about to be ripped off.

Ignoring the odds, relying solely on his own overrated competance as a judge of human nature and the dubious abilities of itinerant bookkeepers to protect him from employee dishonesty, he goes blissfully back to the shop to listen to the tinkle of his cash registers. When the inevitable bolt from the blue finally strikes, he cries out, amazed and disillusioned, that such a tragedy should befall him.

Another source of valuable outside assistance the independent merchant often fails to utilize is that offered by the cash register and other business machine companies. Convinced that the bright young people representing these concerns are solely after his money, he does not give them the time of day and he chooses to continue the use of obsolete cash-receiving equipment, some of which may be real klunkers of no more use than a cigar box for the protection of the cash receipts.

All improvements in the design of cash-receiving and -recording systems are aimed at bettering the effectiveness of internal controls. Whether or not he intends to buy, the proprietor will do well to listen to the sales representative's pitch, for, in addition to knowing the capabilities of his merchandise, he has a good practical knowledge of office procedures and the soft spots that may develop in them. Should the merchant feel that the sales rep's exuberance is leading toward an extravagant expenditure, a word with his accountant can quickly establish the cost effectiveness of the proposal. Meanwhile, the freebies from such an encounter might prove most useful (see Chapter 8).

A whole new generation of office and accounting machines has been born during the past decade, and the capability of this equipment is nothing less than fantastic. Computers and computer applications have been adapted for use by smaller businesses, and computer service bureaus have become almost as plentiful as gas stations. The electronic age has something to offer in the way of increased efficiency, security, and profits for the smart entrepreneur who is willing to look and listen. Unfortunately, too many sales-oriented proprietors with massive mental blocks and acute myopia still persist in regarding all expenditures for bookkeeping and account- ing personnel, procedures, and equipment strictly as money down the rat hole.

A mere listing of all of the sins of omission and commission perpetrated by employers as unwitting accomplices of their employees' thievery would fill a volume several times the size of this one. These sins individually would fall pretty much into the categories herein explored, and collectively they would spell out one huge word—in three-colored neon—NEGLECT! This is a harsh indictment of many struggling and harassed entrepreneurs; but, as has been noted, "they do not realize that loss prevention/asset protection is just another management problem, amenable to solution by the application of standard management principles."[1] Ignorance in and of itself is not neglect. Negligence is the willful disregard of caution and common sense. In all too many cases of embezzlement, the negligence of the employer equals the cupidity of the employee.

If you, dear reader, are an employer or manager of a business, when you go to your office tomorrow take a small piece of paper or a card and write on it, in large capital letters, TNT. Place it where you can see it 50 times a day. The casual observer might wonder idly why you were interested in trinitrotoluene and pass over it without comment. Only you will know that the letters also represent the "chemical" formula for another equally devastating explosive of which *you* could easily be the victim should you fail to heed its warning:

TEMPTATION + NEGLECT = THEFT

NOTE
1. *Crimes Against Business Project; Background, Findings and Recommendations* (AMACOM, 1977).

Part II

SOME
BLACK SHEEP
AND HOW THEY
CLIPPED
THEIR SHEPHERDS

Having taken a close look at embezzlers in general—who they are, why they steal, and how they are assisted by their unwitting employers—it is time to take a closer look at a few of them in particular. All of the events described are based upon actual cases.

To avoid identification of individuals or communities, all proper names used are strictly fictitious, and any resemblance to any person, living or dead, or to any existing community or place is wholly coincidental. Also, further to prevent identification, introductory descriptions of the scene of the crime and the supporting characters are largely fictitious, and, of major importance, some essential details of the modus operandi have been changed or omitted to prevent their being employed by any reader who might be tempted to do so. (Sorry about that.)

5

ONE FOR
THE PRICE
OF TWO

Ask anyone in Crystal City (population 42,723) who was a good lawyer in town, and the odds are 5 to 1 that you would be told that Chauncey Chadwick was right at the top. Poised, affable, conservatively dressed, and still a youngish 39, "Chy" Chadwick radiated the competence and self-confidence that had drawn together a solid and loyal clientele. Though you might hear an occasional grumble about the fees he charged, it would be followed quickly by the avowal that his services were well worth the price of admission. Among his colleagues he was respected, admired, and often envied for both his ability and his success. He had served two terms as president of the Jefferson County Bar Association, and it was generally held inevitable that some day the governor would tap him on the shoulder to fill a vacancy on the local superior court bench.

Chadwick's base of operations was a spacious and gracious suite of offices on the top floor (the fourth) of Crystal City's tallest structure, First Fidelity Bank and Trust Building. The decor of his professionally decorated reception room quickly dispelled any misconception that his fees would be modest, though the soft background music helped somewhat to soothe the realization. Immediately behind the reception room, visible through a pass-through window, was the working area and sacred domain of Betty Belle Bowman, without whose faithful and efficient daily ministrations the Chadwick law offices would grind to a screeching halt. For 11 years, from a cubby-hole office to the present plush suite, Betty Belle had followed the fortunes of Chy Chadwick, had contributed greatly to their rise, and had, in turn, been appreciatively rewarded by her employer.

Her skills were such that she could draft a set of corporation bylaws or probate petitions as well as Chadwick. Only an approving glance from him was necessary before he affixed his signature, and on occasions when he was in a hurry, even that formality was assigned to Betty Belle. It was Betty Belle who got on her employer's back when he was slow in fixing client charges, and it was she who adjusted the bills upward when she thought that he had not charged enough. She did the banking, prepared the checks in payment of office expenses, did the bookkeeping, and made up the annual statement of income and expense that was submitted to accountant Mike Moses for the preparation of income tax returns.

Cynthia Chadwick was truly a dream walking, and her photo on Chy's desk was the object of a thousand loving glances each day. Spoiled rotten by her adoring husband and with not much of a financial IQ, Cynthia did not even try to balance her checkbook, keep track of the household expenses, or pay bills until the third notice from creditors. She dressed like a fashion plate and, being childless, she spent her mornings on the golf course and her afternoons at the bridge table. To get a grip on his domestic financial affairs, Chauncey Chadwick finally had all his household bills mailed directly to his office and arranged with the bank for courtesy notification when Cynthia's checking account was overdrawn, which was frequently. It was, of course, on Betty Belle's capable shoulders that the burden fell to attend to the nitty-gritty, including a duty that she rather relished—the review of Cynthia's hefty department store and credit card statements. Out of her busiest schedule, she made time for a thorough inspection.

It was during his third year in practice that Betty Belle first walked into Chadwick's office and applied for a job. Prior to that time his secretarial needs had been filled by a more-or-less satisfactory series of part-time workers. He had long looked forward to the day when he could afford full-time help, though that day had not yet arrived, he felt, when Betty Belle called upon him. But when he found that—"for personal reasons"—she had just left the prestigious law offices of Mumper, Bumper, and Thumper, where she had been old Martin Mumper's personal secretary, he knew he was confronted with *the* opportunity of his young life. Before he could marshal his doubts as to her affordability, she volunteered that her starting salary requirements could be tempered to meet the financial realities of his practice. Delighted beyond words, he hired her on the spot. ("Just wait 'til word gets back to the exalted firm of M B & T that she is working for *me*," he mused.) Within 48 hours she had settled in as though she had been in the position for 48 months.

Except that she was a pleasant, tireless, and efficient secretary, Chadwick learned really very little over the next 11 years about Betty Belle Bowman, the person. She kept her personal life strictly to herself. She had no local relatives, only a couple of sisters back East somewhere, and her only evident social life was limited to spasmodic attendance at church, where she occasionally served as relief organist. Though she was not an unattractive woman, she gave no evidence of prior or current romantic interest. Apparently, Betty Belle's sole love was for music, and this love she pursued with vigor. In her modest home stood a huge grand piano, and the rest of her living room was crowded with stereophonic equipment and cabinets holding literally hundreds of records and tapes. During the symphony and opera seasons, she made the 400-mile round trip to "the city" almost every weekend. Truly, it seemed that music was her consuming passion.

It was in the spring, shortly after April 15, that Chauncy Chadwick called his friend and accountant, Mike Moses, and asked if they could have lunch together. Over the coffee cups after lunch, Chadwick broached a subject that had been bothering him.

"Mike, I've got a problem. I went over my tax returns very carefully, and it really bugs me that I am taking in so much money, and have been for several years, and yet have so damned little to show for it. Don't tell me that I am living too high on the hog—I know it. And I run an expensive office; I could almost live on what I spend to keep up my library alone. I have thought about it until it's driving me bananas, and I can't figure where the money goes, or how I can stop it. I've waited until you were over your tax-season rush, but now I want you to move in on me and go over my operation from top to bottom. Dig into everything and don't worry about the cost. I've got to get some answers, and damned quick!"

"O.K., Chy. Can do. First let me ask you a few questions."

"Shoot."

"First, what is your procedure for paying the monthly bills?"

"Well, you know there are two kinds of bills—for the office and for the house. Cynthia can't manage money, so all of the household bills come to the office."

Mike nodded.

"Just before the tenth of the month, Betty Belle goes through all the bills to see that they are O.K. and makes out the checks. Then she brings me the bills and the checks on both the business and the personal accounts, and I sign the checks and she mails them out. We've always done it that way."

"Do you go over the bills pretty thoroughly yourself?"

"H-m-m-m—not really. I'm usually so busy that I just look to see whom we're paying and how much. Anyway, Betty Belle has given them a good going over. Maybe I should look at them more carefully, but I generally don't."

"How about your bank statements and canceled checks? Do you examine them when they first come in?"

"Oh, not regularly, maybe every other month or so.

Betty Belle checks them off to see that all the deposits got on and how much we have left in the bank. She generally asks me if I want to look at them, and sometimes I do."

"All right. Now, at the end of the year, when Betty Belle makes up the statement for the tax returns, do you go over the books with her so that you know what's going on, what the expenses are, and how much it is costing you to run the office and your house?"

"Lord, no! I haven't the foggiest idea what's in those books. They're all Greek to me, and besides, I hate figures! Look, Mike, don't ask me any more questions. Maybe I'm doing everything wrong. Just get started on it as soon as you can. You can work in the library, and Betty Belle will tell you about everything. Can you be there the first of the week?"

Mike thought for a moment before replying, and then spoke slowly and carefully.

"Look, Chy. I want a chance to look through things a bit when Betty Belle isn't there. I'm not saying that anything is wrong or that I even suspect that anything is wrong, but that's the way I want to do it. Can you be there, say at 8:30 Saturday morning, and is there any chance that she might come in the office while I'm there? Oh, yes, and by the way, is she bonded?"

Chadwick bristled.

"No, she's not bonded, and no, she won't be there—she's going to a concert in the city—and yes, I can be there if that's what you want. I think you're way out in left field, but I'll go along with you. You'd better come up with something concrete, or I'll nail your hide to the barn door!"

"Take it easy, Chy! Everything's probably all right—I hope it is—but there's no need to upset Betty Belle by

42

having me snoop around while she's there, so just keep it to yourself until we've had a chance to look around. O.K.?"

On the following Monday afternoon just after five o'clock, as Betty Belle was finishing clearing her desk, the reception room door opened and in stepped two deputy sheriffs, one male, one female.

Said the man,

"Miss Bowman, we have a warrant for your arrest on charges of embezzlement and forgery."

While the deputy recited the Miranda warning, his fellow officer stepped into the inner office where she stood quietly beside the suspect's chair. As the reading finished, she said quietly,

"You'll have to come with us. I'll help you get your coat and purse."

Betty Belle sat quietly for a moment staring at the floor, then rose slowly, shaking her head.

"I guess I should have expected it," she whispered. "I'll go with you."

Three weeks later, Bruce Byers, district attorney of Jefferson County, sat back in his chair and regarded the pile of documents on his desk that Mike Moses, just departed, had deposited there. Packs of canceled checks, sheaves of bank statements, credit card and department store bills, and photostats of numerous other documents made up the pile. On top lay Mike's 17-page report of the findings of his examination of the records of Chauncey Chadwick, attorney at law. Byers reached for the report, and flipping through the first 16 pages, noted the detailed listing of nearly 400 separate illegal acts of Betty Belle

Bowman, concisely summarized on the last page of the report:

17 canceled checks in hand bearing forged signatures	$ 4,391.07
134 missing canceled checks, presumably destroyed, for which photostatic copies were obtained from bank microfilm records, all bearing forged signatures	48,308.90
238 forged credit card charges made by use of duplicate credit cards obtained by forged requests	8,802.61
	$61,502.58

Analysis of yearly defalcation totals:

19—	$ 635.00
19—	3,031.31
19—	6,840.42
19—	9,730.03
19—	14,961.67
19—	19,008.90
19—(4 months)	7,295.25
	$61,502.58

Five weeks later in his chambers, Superior Court Judge Roger Robbins adjusted his glasses and resumed reading the presentencing report of the probation officer.

"She still insists that probably over $40,000 of the embezzled funds were lost gambling at Lake Mañana. We

44

question the validity of this contention, since our interrogations have disclosed that she has only a limited knowledge of gambling procedures, or of locations and arrangements of gambling casinos, or of lodging and meal accommodations at Lake Mañana. . . ."

The judge gazed out the window.

"Hmmm," he mused. "I wonder where she's got it stashed away."

The black-and-white patrol car bearing the seal of the Jefferson County Sheriff's Department pulled away from the admission gate at State Prison for Women as Betty Belle Bowman began her first day of two-to-five-years' imprisonment on seven counts of grand theft to which she had pleaded guilty.

On the shady patio of Verde Vista Retirement Manor, retired attorney Martin Mumper and his wife of 52 years, Myrtle, sat reading the local morning paper. A short paragraph on an inside page noted the departure of Betty Belle Bowman to her new residence.

"Ya' know, Myrt? One of the smartest things I ever did was to get that note and mortgage on her house when I caught her stealing from *me*."

He paused and chuckled.

"And I wouldn't be surprised if that young whipper-snapper didn't help to pay me back!"

6

PARALYSIS OF THE GLUTEUS MAXIMUS

Most people can still remember the pleasant days before the energy crisis. Gasoline was selling in the 30-cent bracket, and frequent gas wars made a profitable game of driving slowly down the street on Sunday afternoon, with the kids in the back trying to spot the sign with the lowest prices. About the only crossroads in the country without one or more filling stations were way out in the middle of nowhere. All America needed was another 100,000 gas stations!

Some of these establishments were impressive, brilliantly lighted complexes called superservices catering

46

to the every need of the traveler and his car. Operators and employees were courteous and efficient, and neatness and cleanliness were standard operating practices.

The vast majority of gasoline outlets, however, were far less pretentious, and an unfortunately large number of them were rather sorry examples of free enterprise at its worst. With ramshackle buildings with peeling paint and grease all over everywhere, filthy rest rooms, and junky yards, they were disgraceful blights on their neighborhoods. As though wanting to be in complete harmony with the general decor of his establishment, the proprietor also dressed and groomed to match his surroundings.

Before we go too far with our condemnation of the poor fellow, however, we should understand that he was afflicted with a fairly common but very peculiar disease, *paralysis of the gluteus maximus* (often vulgarly referred to as "lead in the butt"), which kept him in a sitting position and prevented locomotion except for the most urgent reasons. Scorned by the major oil companies, who did not wish to have their logos and colors displayed amid such surroundings, our friend and his colleagues were generally dependent for their merchandise upon small petroleum distributors marketing off-brand products, products sometimes actually produced by the same finicky major refiners.

A charming young gentleman, whom we shall call Bud, greatly enjoyed his job as driver of a gasoline truck for an independent distributor. Among other things, he liked the open air and the camaraderie and salty discourse with his customers. When he drove into the station yard and stopped by the fill pipe, the conversation might go something like this:

"Hi, Butch, ya old bastard! How many today?"

"Aw, give me 300, Bud—that's all I can pay for."

(Yes, he was on the COD list.)

"O.K., Butch. D'ya want to read the meter?"

"Naw, go ahead. I'm tired."

When our tired friend had paid for 300 gallons, and the two had exchanged a few friendly parting insults, Bud got in his truck and pulled out of the station. Down the road a way, he stopped, removed a little tin sheet from his sales book, and, with a voided invoice as a matrix, filled in the last three copies of his sales invoice for the 280 gallons of gasoline actually delivered.

Before the day was over, Bud had repeated the process with other tired customers until he had collected money for more than 100 gallons that he had not delivered. When he checked into the plant that night, his delivery invoice copies agreed exactly with his out-and-in truck meter readings; his cash turned in balanced, of course, with his recorded total cash sales. No one except Bud knew how much extra cash remained in his pocket. At the then-wholesale price of gasoline and Bud's current wages, he had tripled his take-home pay. No wonder he liked his job.

Unfortunately for Bud, one of his customers was the father of a bright young girl who was taking high school bookkeeping and was fascinated with figures. She prevailed upon her father to let her try to install some semblance of order in his record keeping, and in the process, discovered that he was buying much more gasoline than he was selling. Armed with a sheaf of paid invoices, the girl went to the distributor's plant, where a quick comparison with the plant invoice copies quickly disclosed Bud's little scheme.

PARALYSIS OF THE GLUTEUS MAXIMUS

The distributor called in his accountant. After the audit was completed, he refunded over $6,000 to his customers. Bud had already been fired. He was not bonded, and his employer refused to prosecute for fear that publicity would damage his business.

7

"OOPS!
I GOOFED!"

In the months immediately following World War II, as many now-retired merchants will never forget, it was an uphill battle to keep merchandise on the shelves and satisfy the demands of customers who thought, now that the war was over, they should instantly be able to get all of the things they had long been doing without. The GIs were streaming home by the tens of thousands, getting married, establishing new households, and procreating like crazy. The shoddy substitutes born of war-time necessity were ready for the dump, and money was in hand for quality replacements. All of the makings were present for booming prosperity, except for one minor problem—there was nothing to sell.

In industrial areas, manufacturers, overexpanded for the war effort, were frantically struggling to convert from bombers to bathtubs, each hoping to get his share of the frenzied action. Small new companies, often capitalized mainly by the guts and grit of a returned veteran, were springing up to produce gadgets and gimmicks previously unheard of by the civilian population. And out in the territory, salesmen were beginning to call on merchants again, optimistically offering to supply merchandise that they fervently hoped their companies could deliver.

There was nothing about Brown's Hardware to distinguish it from 10,000 other small-town hardware stores scattered across the face of the nation. Located on Main Street, two blocks from the center of town, it had the same double-door-center entrance, flanked by the same two shallow display windows, and protected by the same roll-down awning that marked the facades of a myriad of its counterparts. Normally, the show windows would have been crowded with merchandise: shotguns and shells, rods and lures for the sportsman; irons and toasters and percolators, pots and pans and dishes for the housewife; but during the war the displays had been limited to bundles of baling wire, shovels and pitchforks, cultivator sweeps and tractor parts. Thank God for the farmers! Without them, and the priority status accorded agriculture and agricultural suppliers as essentials to the war effort, Bert Brown and thousands like him would have had to close their doors and go to work in the shipyards.

Shortly after Pearl Harbor, when Bert's bookkeeper left to join the Waves, Bert's wife, Bobbie, was "recalled to active duty," to take over that department for the duration. With business dwindling and help hard to come by, Brown's Hardware had become literally a mom and pop store. Now, as soon as it was all over, Bobbie immediately put in for an "honorable discharge" and was replaced by a returning aircraft parts clerk, Judy Jackson, a little rusty but still a competent bookkeeper.

Working day and night to "borrow, beg, or steal" merchandise from any and every possible source of supply, Bert had little time nor did it appear necessary to look over Judy's shoulder at her work. He was on the telephone hours on end running down every lead that might produce something to sell; soon, in dribbles and dabs, the goods began to trickle in. With the small flow of stock, however, there was a veritable flood of invoices, mostly from companies never heard of before, full of errors and smeared with back-order stamps. Judy was literally up to her elbows in work, checking, correcting, and filing invoices and preparing checks for payment.

Judy needed her job. She *had* to keep busy. Though she loved him dearly, when little Joey raced to greet her each evening, his growing resemblance to big Joe stabbed her in the heart; when she fled to her bedroom, there was Joe's picture in his flying togs forever grinning at her. Homecoming was not the best hour of her day.

Though Joe's pension and the Social Security survivor's benefit nicely augmented her salary and assured a comfortable living for her and Joey, she still harbored a horrible fear that sometime she might not be able to work, the pension and the Social Security might be withdrawn, and she and her child would be destitute. Most often the obsession peaked just as she tried to go to sleep, and then she almost wished that she were back on the night shift at the aircraft factory. It was there, at the first, that she would often dream that the shiny part she was handling might go into a plane that Joe would fly. If only Joe were here. If only she could feel a little more secure.

It was about the middle of the following July that Judy came down with summer flu. After she had hacked and coughed around the store for a couple of days, Bert Brown sent her home with instructions to stay there until she was well. When she protested vigorously that she could not afford to get behind with her work and that financially she could not afford the time off, Bert assured her that Bobbie would pinch-hit for her and that her salary would be continued. Reluctantly, she departed.

Bobbie was opening the mail, and Bert was at his nearby desk making some telephone calls.

"Bert, look at this." Bobbie handed him a letter.

It was on the stationery of the Western Widget Company ("We have the most complete stock of widgets in the West"). It read:

Mrs. Judy Jackson, Bookkeeper
Brown's Hardware
Centralville, Calizona

Dear Mrs. Jackson:

Please don't feel sorry that you "goofed." We did, too, for we should have caught your error.

Enclosed find our check in the amount of $45.00 in refund of the overpayment.

Thank you for calling it to our attention.

Sincerely,
WESTERN WIDGET COMPANY
Fred Forrest
Office Manager

"Well, so what?" Bert handed the letter and check back to Bobbie. "She made a mistake, and she got the money back. I'm just glad to see that she's on the ball. Put it in the bank."

Bobbie shrugged, and Bert went out in the store to wait on a customer.

Three days later Bobbie called to Bert as he passed the office door.

"Bert, we've got another one of those letters. This one is from General Gadget & Supply, and it has a check for $81 in it."

Bert took the letter and sat down at his desk. Presently he said, "Look up the statement and the invoice—and look up the stub of the check that paid it."

Bobbie shuffled through the files for the papers and got the checkbook from the safe and laid them on Bert's desk. Together they studied the documents. The one invoice attached to the statement and the statement itself were for $109.17, but the check stub showed that the check had been drawn for $190.17, a transposition error of $81.00. Reading Bert's mind, Bobbie turned again to the file cabinet and retrieved the statement of Western Widget. It, too, had one invoice attached for the sum of $127.80, but the check had been issued for $172.80, another transposition error of $45, which Western Widget had refunded.

"I thought you checked these yourself before you signed the checks," said Bobbie quietly.

"I *always* do!" Bert was sharp and emphatic. "But I guess I must have slipped up on these—too much on my mind."

He paused and thought.

"Hey, wait a minute! A month or two ago I *did* catch

one of them. I showed it to Judy, and she just laughed and said, 'Oh, I sure goofed!' and then she made out another check."

Bert and Bobbie sat looking at each other, exercising their ESP. Finally, Bobbie said, "Yup! I think so, too. I'll go to work." And she did.

When Bert got back from the country a couple of hours later, Bobbie showed him a list of 12 more similar "errors" over the past three months, totaling over $700—"and I'm not sure that's all of them either."

Robert Reynolds, C.P.A., sat holding a columnar paper with a list of items and figures totaling over $2,600, a sum that was unbelievable to his client who faced him across the desk shaking his head.

"I can't believe it, Bob. In just seven months! But what good did it do her? Who would cash the checks; they were made out to the store?"

Reynolds laughed.

"That's easy, Bert. *You* did—out of the cash sales money."

It was a solemn circle of faces that surrounded the table in attorney Paul Patterson's library. In addition to Patterson, present were Judy Jackson, Bert and Bobbie Brown, Bob Reynolds, and Monte Moreno, a deputy from the district attorney's office. The silence was broken only by Judy's constant nose blowing. Finally Bert spoke.

"I've made up my mind. I'm *not* going to prosecute her, and I'm *not* going to fire her. She says that she put all the money in her savings account and she will pay me back. I think that she has learned her lesson—I hope she has—and so she can just go on back to work. But, Judy,

I'm telling you, if you ever try any funny business again, I'll see that they put you in jail and throw the key away!"

He paused, then started to rise.

"And that's the way it's going to be!"

8

THE CATTY-CORNERED CASH REGISTER

Noel Nickerson never heard the shot that crashed out of the jungle and into his chest, knocking him sprawling face down in the filthy muck of a rice paddy. Six weeks later, when next he opened his eyes, he lay in the intensive-care ward of a stateside naval hospital, draped in tubes, punctured with needles, and surrounded by a galaxy of blinking lights and quivering dials. Startled and confused, he lapsed momentarily back into semiconsciousness until his addled brain could sort things out a bit. After another nine months or so of treatment, including psychotherapy, he was released from the hospital and discharged from the Marine Corps. Bitter and vengeful, he returned to his home.

His bitterness was monumental. It was an all-consuming hate. It gnawed at his guts during the day and deviled his dreams at night.

He hated the top brass of his own military who had consorted with the native politicians, scratching each other's backs and crossing each other's palms.

He hated the greedy among his own comrades who had sold their arms and ammunition on the black market knowing that the material would immediately fall into the hands of the enemy.

He hated the complacent civilians back home and, particularly, the long-haired draft resistors who had paraded across the campuses chanting, "Hell no, we won't go!"

But, most of all, he hated the bungling politicians who had gotten the nation involved in a bloody war they did not even try to win!

There was no peace for Noel Nickerson. Each endless day was like the endless yesterday. Slumped hour after hour before the inane boob tube, unresponsive to his mother's gentle and understanding concern, and totally disinterested in the world beyond his walls, Noel nursed his bitterness and let time pass him by—month after month after month.

"I think he's beginning to come out of it," said Noel "Nick" Nickerson, Sr. to his friend Dave Dodds as they sat on a couple of sacks of grain in the store of Dodds Feed and Seed Company.

"A few days ago he said he guessed he ought to do something about looking for a job, but he was afraid nobody would hire him. He hasn't much strength, and he gets awfully short of breath if he exerts too much. If he could just find some kind of light work, regardless of what it paid him, I think it would be real good for him."

"Nick, I just might be able to use him," Dodds ventured. "I don't get around as good as I used to, and I really need someone to wait on the truck scales and chase around out in the mill looking after the unloading and checking on the men getting out the orders. When we are busy, he could help handle the sales up front, and maybe I could get away once in awhile. Send him around. I'd like to talk to him."

No one could tell whether Noel Nickerson liked his job or not. He faithfully performed his duties, proficiently and promptly, but devoid of any show of enthusiasm or interest. He spoke when he was spoken to and volunteered nothing. To the men in the mill, he was an oddball, and conversation stopped when he came around. To the customers, he was courteous and helpful, but, used to Dave's affable chatter, they found him a little strange and distant. And to Dave?

"Well, I just let him alone. As long as he does his work, I'll have no complaints. It would be nice, though, if he would just loosen up a bit."

The cash register out in the store was a dilly. It should have been drawing Social Security! Ancient when Dave opened his first modest feed store 30 years ago, it had not improved with age. It did have a cash drawer, and it did have a recording tape and a bell that rang when the drawer was opened, but that was about all that could be said for its usefulness. Its brass was tarnished; the glass in the little window on the customer's side, where the numbers popped up, was cracked and ready to fall out. The cracked glass had bothered Noel; he was afraid someone would get cut on it, so he taped the crack with a narrow strip of masking tape. Dave noted and approved.

A few weeks later, as they were standing together in the store, Noel broached a subject to which apparently he had given considerable thought.

"Dave, would you mind if I moved the cash register a little bit? The way it sets on the counter, when you are waiting on a customer out on the floor, you have to go clear around in back of the counter to ring up a sale. If it could be moved to the end of the counter and set catty-cornered, you could work it from both sides, and it would save a lot of time. What do you think?"

Dave was flabbergasted. That was the longest utterance that Noel had made since he had started to work, and the first suggestion that he had made to improve ways of doing things. Maybe he was beginning to snap out of it. "O.K., Noel. We'll give it a try. It might work fine. Just be sure you don't turn it so far that somebody could get at it when you were not watching."

Greg Gomez was a persistent little guy. Among the first Chicanos to break into the sales force of one of the big cash register companies, he was determined to show his Anglo peers that he could sell with the best of them. Not only did he know his merchandise down to the last transistor, but he was a tiger when he got on the trail of a good prospect. His quiet sincerity, his unfailing courtesy, and his broad smile assured that his persistence never gave offense. Over a period of many months, he had patiently beaten a broad path to Dave Dodds's door; and over occasional cups of coffee, he and Dave's accountant had conspired toward the upgrading of Dave's accounting system, the heart of which would be a versatile new cash register. To date, their progress had not been notable. Dave was a hard nut to crack.

Greg stood patiently in the store waiting for Dave to finish with a customer so that he could give him the new monthly edition of his sales pitch. Casually he watched as Noel accepted a $10 bill from a customer, rang up the sale, and returned to the customer a $1 bill and some change. As Noel went to wait on the next customer, Greg stepped closer to the cash register. Glancing at the little window where the figures showed, he noted that the strip of tape with which Noel had repaired the cracked glass obscured most of the left half of the dollar figure—he could not tell whether it was an 8 or a 3. The cents figures, 17 cents, were clearly visible. At the angle at which the register sat on the counter, he could not get a better look without appearing obvious.

When Dave was finally free, and Noel had gone out to the mill, Greg asked Dave to open the compartment in the register where the tape was stored; he wanted to get the serial number, he said. Grudgingly, Dave complied.

There was no $8.17 sale on the tape; but, four sales back, there was a $3.17 sale. Greg stepped around to the customer's side of the register and leaned over the counter.

"Please come around here, Mr. Dodds. Now watch."

Stepping back to the front of the register, Greg rang an $8 figure and then a $3 figure.

"Now lift up that piece of tape, Mr. Dodds."

Again he rang the same figures.

"Well, I'll be damned," said Dave. "I see what you mean—a neat $5 bill for his pocket whenever he made an $8 sale!"

"Screw you, Judge!" Noel screamed. "Screw all of you. Yeah, I did it. I clipped the old goat for thirty or forty bucks a day—him and his dirty money grabbing—I wish

I'd have broke him! Go ahead, throw me in jail. It makes no difference to me. They should have let me die in Nam. I'm no damned good to myself or anybody else. Go on, get it over with!"

Judge Abel Adams looked gravely down from the bench.

"This is a sad day for me, Noel. I've known you and your family all of your life, and I know what you have been through. It was tough—real tough. However, that does not excuse what you have done, and that cannot be overlooked."

He paused.

"It is the judgment of this court that you serve one to three years in State Penitentiary. However, in view of the circumstances, sentence is hereby suspended, and you are placed on five years' probation provided that you return immediately to the Veterans Hospital for extended psychiatric treatment. It has all been arranged for you, and you are to report there tomorrow. Good luck, son!"

Dave Dodds and Greg Gomez walked silently down the courthouse steps. At the bottom, Dave turned and looked smilingly at Greg.

"O.K., wise guy! You'd do *anything* to sell a cash register, wouldn't you?"

Greg smiled back.

"Si, Señor. When do you want it delivered?"

9

WATERING DOWN THE WATER WORKS

No fairer or richer land exists on the face of the earth than the San Geronimo Valley of Central Calizona. One hundred miles in width and over 200 miles in length, its millions of fertile acres nourish the roots of an unparalleled assortment of prolific trees and vines, shrubs and grasses. Its insatiable thirst slaked by never-failing rivers from the snow-capped Sierra Ponderosa, and blessed with long summer months of brilliant sunshine, the valley pours out its bountiful and endless flood of food and fiber to feed and clothe millions around the world. By rail and freeway, and even by air, its precious produce is shuttled, day and night and through-out the year, to awaiting markets.

The lawn-level floor of the valley is laced and cross-laced with hundreds of miles of concrete rivers, and the foothill valleys of the Sierra Ponderosa are dotted with man-made lakes, all to hold and distribute efficiently the precious melt of winter snows. Here modern farmers have met and conquered a perverse Nature, ended the perennial cycle of flood and drought, and produced a verdant expanse, which its residents with pride and justification affectionately call "God's Greenhouse."

Scattered broadly across the valley, a hundred or more small communities, with populations of a few hundred to a few thousand, serve as the political, commercial, and social centers essential to the produc-tion and marketing of the annual outpouring of neighbor-ing farms, vineyards, orchards, and groves. Typically, these are solid, conservative, and prosperous little cities of modest homes, modest businesses, and modest people. Because each surrounding area of production requires the support of only so many merchants, bankers, doctors, teachers, and mechanics, these communities grow slowly and change very little over the years. Their life-style is pleasant, congenial, and easygoing; their activities closely cycled to the tempo of the growing and the harvest seasons.

Such a little city is Vinland, close to the foothills, originally populated by Scandinavian and Germanic settlers, and the home of, naturally, the Vinland Vikings, consistent winners in the high school football league. The 9,000 or so souls inhabiting Vinland are about equally located on the two sides of the railroad track bisecting the city. On the south side are the modest homes and small stores of the Hispanic people who work in the surrounding vineyards and groves, in the fruit-packing plants that line the tracks, and at the winery on the outskirts of town. North of the railroad lies the small but bustling business district; and, fanning out behind it, the neatly kept streets and homes of the Anglo white- and blue-collar workers of Vinland extend to the city limits, where the city ends abruptly, confronted on all sides by orchards and vineyards.

Adjacent to the business district, two city blocks are covered by the green lawns and shady grove of Central Park, which is also the site of the municipal swimming pool, the Boy Scout log cabin, the Veterans Memorial Building, and City Hall. Immediately behind City Hall towers the water tank, shining with fresh aluminum paint and bearing in huge letters the legend, "Home of the Vinland Vikings."

Architecturally, City Hall could best be described as "Late Depression WPA." It is a sturdy, gray brick, no-nonsense, H-shaped structure, good for many years to come. Its right and left wings are occupied respectively by the fire department and the police department, while the center section houses the general municipal office, the city court, and the city council chambers.

Administratively, the day-to-day business of the City of Vinland has been conducted by two full-time employees: the city clerk, Velma Volkman, and the city engineer, Larry Larson, who shared opposite ends of the large central office. Though their respective official duties were distinctly segregated, practical necessity required at times that each cover for the other in the office. When Larry was out, Velma could and did issue building permits, and similarly when Velma was out, Larry received and receipted water bill payments. For many years both had served at the pleasure of successive city councils, had kept their noses clean politically, and had projected a good image of courteous, efficient, and helpful public servants.

Sprinkles of gray were beginning to show in Velma Volkman's dark hair, a fact noted with no surprise by her friends and co-workers. Divorced at an early age with no means of support other than her own efforts, Velma's life had been a hard and constant struggle to provide a home and care for her husky son, Victor. She felt totally inadequate trying to be both mother and father to the boy and, in compensation, from his early childhood had lavished upon her "little Vicki" every present and pleasure he demanded. As a result, nearing 18, he was an insolent young slob draining his mother's financial and emotional resources, and kept out of jail only by the reluctance of the local police to bring further worry and grief to Velma. On one occasion it was gruff old Judge Axel Anderson who had said with brutal frankness to Velma, "That boy of yours is just like a two-year-old bull calf still on the tit!"

Velma had fled sobbing.

It was in late July when the auditors arrived for the annual examination of the books and records of the City of Vinland. As a veteran of many years of coping with the peculiarities and pickinesss of auditors, Velma could take in stride the annoyances and disruptions of their visitation. Year after year the audit reports had given her a clean bill of health and even, in professionally restrained wording, had commented favorably on the neatness and accuracy of the municipal records that she maintained. This year, however, was slightly different; Velma was a little concerned. The firm of accountants that had performed the audit for many years had been replaced by a new firm selected by the city council on the theory that "new brooms sweep clean" and that change in and of itself is often beneficial. Velma went mentally over and over every account on the books, repeatedly reassuring herself that the new auditors, too, would find nothing amiss.

Less than two months ago, Paul Parker had received his bachelor of business administration degree from State University and had gone on the payroll of Blake and Lake, Accountants and Auditors, as a junior accountant. Now, as assistant to Lloyd Lake and on his first audit assignment, he was enthusiastic and eager to turn in a perfect performance as a cub auditor.

The customers' ledger of the Vinland City Water Department was a huge book, not too thick but with extra-large pages. Arranged by streets, each line listed a customer's name and street address, followed by 12 double columns in which the billing debits and the payment credits were entered for a full year. It was a formidible-looking volume—Paul had seen nothing like it in his accounting classes—yet, when its workings were explained, it was seen to be practical and logical, the only alternative to a computerized system, which a small city like Vinland could not afford.

Paul's first task assigned by Lloyd Lake was to prove the footings of the water ledger and trace the balances to the general ledger. It was dull, tedious, monotonous work, and after two days of steady labor, Paul began to wonder if this was a sample of the supposed glamor he had always associated with auditing. And the end was not in sight. His next step would be to test-check the postings to the ledger of several thousand receipted water bill stubs.

It was in midmorning of his third day of checking water bill stubs that Paul threw down his pencil in disgust and started for the door.

"I've got to get some fresh air or I'll go nuts," he explained to Velma Volkman. "Back in a few minutes."

Walking leisurely to the corner drugstore two blocks away, Paul entered the pay telephone booth and called his home office in a neighboring city. When he had Lloyd Lake on the line, he began,

"Mr. Lake, I'm calling from a pay phone downtown. I've got a problem. I have a receipted water bill stub for an account that is not on the ledger. What shall I do?"

"Did you say anything to Mrs. Volkman?" Lake asked quickly.

"No. I thought I ought to talk to you first. She might think I was stupid if I asked her. I've looked and looked, but it just plain isn't there."

"Good! Don't say anything to her. I'll be out there just before noon. Lay that stub on your desk so I can see it when I get there, but don't say anything to me about it. Write down the customer's name and address, and put it in your pocket. Then we'll go to lunch together and discuss it."

After lunch the two men drove to the address Paul had noted. It was located in a small subdivision opened about six years before by the extension of two existing streets for two blocks into a vineyard. Thirty-two nice homes had been built during the six years, in the 1200 and 1300 blocks of Peach and Cherry Streets. The address they had been looking for was 1216 Peach Street.

Returning to City Hall, Lloyd Lake started Paul on the audit of building permits, while he began casually to review Paul's working papers on the water department.

From time to time he flipped through the pages of the water ledger. Definitely, there were no accounts for any of the houses in the new subdivision. As he worked, he was aware that Velma Volkman was watching him closely. Finally, she spoke, rather petulantly.

"When will you be through with the water ledger? I'm getting way behind with my posting. The other auditors did the whole water department in a couple of days, and you have tied me up five days already!"

"Sorry about that," Lloyd quietly replied. "If we have good luck, we should finish with it today. It always takes more time the first time around."

An hour or so later, after final instructions to Paul and a friendly good-bye to Velma, Lloyd departed. Instead of returning to his office, he drove to the farm equipment store of Vinland's mayor, Steve Swensen. Closeted in Steve's office, Lloyd took from his briefcase the water bill stub for 1216 Peach Street, gave it to Steve, and explained his findings. In conclusion, he said, "So, at an average of about $5 per month for each of the 32 houses, that means a loss of over $150 per month that we are reasonably sure of. Maybe she can come up with an explanation, but I doubt it very much."

At five o'clock that afternoon, the five members of the city council of Vinland, together with accountant Lloyd Lake, assembled in the office of Roy Rhinehart, city attorney. Said Rinehart, "I told Velma that we had to have an emergency meeting of the council at 5:30 and for her to be here with her notebook at that time. Before she gets here, Mr. Lake, our auditor, has something to tell us about."

As Lloyd talked, the water bill stub was passed from hand to hand; when he had finished, the incredulous members of the council questioned him at length. Finally, convinced, they sat stunned and silent.

Promptly at 5:30, Velma entered the office smiling pleasantly. When she spotted Lloyd Lake, her smile vanished and her eyes widened—she certainly had not expected to see him there! After she had seated herself and as she fumbled in her purse for her pen, Roy Rhinehart addressed her.

"Velma, before we start the meeting, will you tell us what this is?"

He handed her the water bill stub. Swiftly, color faded from her face as she regarded the bit of paper. Glancing defiantly at Lake, she finally answered.

"Why, that's just a water bill stub—nothing wrong with it that I can see. What's this all about anyway?"

Rinehart nodded toward Lake, who quietly said, "There is no account in the water ledger for that address."

Velma countered belligerently, "You mean you couldn't find it! You and that stupid kid you've got working for you couldn't find anything!"

Her eyes swept boldly around the room.

"That's right," said Lloyd evenly. "We couldn't find it."

Then looking squarely at Velma, "And we couldn't find ledger accounts for the other 31 houses in that subdivision, either!"

Velma's face was ashen. Snatching her handkerchief from her purse, she jammed it against her mouth in a vain effort to control the sobs that erupted violently. When at last the tempest had passed, she sat looking pleadingly from face to face. As gently as possible, Roy Rhinehart resumed speaking.

"Velma, Mr. Lake estimates that between $9,000 and $10,000 are missing from the water account. . . ."

He was abruptly cut off.

"Oh, that's crazy! I didn't take. . . ."

She caught herself, paused for a moment, and then finished weakly, "I didn't think it was that much."

Again she was shaken by sobs.

Rhinehart reached for his telephone, dialed the police department, and asked for the chief.

"Joe, this is Roy. Come on over now."

As the solemn group awaited the arrival of the chief of police, Lloyd Lake said quietly, "Mrs. Volkman. It would help us—and help you, too—if you would tell us where you keep the missing ledger accounts."

Absently, she replied, "They're under the blotter pad on my desk."

When the provable shortage in the accounts of the City of Vinland had reached $15,000, Mayor Steve Swensen ordered the firm of Blake and Lake to stop their audit effort. The city clerk was bonded for only $15,000, and since there was no possibility of restitution, the cost of further investigation to satisfy idle curiosity was not justified.

The missing water ledger sheets, carefully maintained, had disclosed a total of 61 meter locations, all on the extreme edges of the city, from which funds had been diverted, some for as long as nine years. Additionally, a book of building permit application forms was found in the back of a drawer in Velma's desk that reflected her "helpful" collection of nearly $1,000 in unrecorded permit fees when the city engineer was out of the office.

STICKY FINGERS

Pursuant to state law providing mandatory imprisonment for the theft of public funds, Velma Volkman was sentenced to three to five years in the state women's penitentiary, and at her request she began immediately to serve her time.

A month later, Victor "Vicki" Volkman, at the request of his guardian grandparents, was sent to state forestry camp as an incorrigible minor.

10

HE NEEDED
NEW GLASSES

For a town the size of San Poco, Valley Furniture and Appliance was a large establishment; in fact, it would have been a sizable store in a community with five times the population of San Poco. Its cavernous showroom covered half a city block, and its solid front of plate glass display windows alone held enough merchandise to furnish fully a half dozen homes. The bane and bugbear of competitors for 50 miles around, "Valley" plastered the billboards, saturated the airwaves, and filled the newsprint of the area with its persuasive messages. And the customers came in droves!

From its bargain basement to the deluxe balcony area, the store offered merchandise to fit every purse and preference, and its salespeople were authorized to wheel and deal to the end that no prospect with any degree of solvency was allowed to leave the premises empty-handed. Price tag figures were strictly points of departure for fast-moving negotiations involving down payments, trade-ins, and contract terms, all leading hopefully to a final figure satisfactory to the customer and profitable to Valley Furniture and Appliance.

Se Habla Español signs were prominently displayed in show windows and on the sales floor, and the goodly representation of Chicano personnel on the sales force and in the office assured the appreciative and loyal patronage of the area's large Spanish-speaking populace. The majority of these people did not have checking accounts and faithfully appeared at the office, particularly on Saturdays, to pay their installment payments in cash. Floor salesclerks were ever alert to take advantage of this periodic transmigration through the store to expose their old customers to new and enticing merchandise. For sure, Valley held its Hispanic patrons in highest esteem.

Eddie Epstein was a good operator. He had parlayed a roadside secondhand store into a multimillion-dollar-a-year business, and in the process had made very few mistakes. He was not a highly educated man—his schooling had been cut short by the Korean War—but he had been liberally endowed with the genes of common sense, hard work, and the ability to turn a quick dollar. There were times when, during reflective moments, Eddie would shake his head in disbelief that he had prospered so well; when others sought to compliment him on his achievements, he would modestly protest that it was "no big deal. I'm just a little guy trying to make a living."

There was a time when Eddie carried all the vital statistics of his business in his head or on the back of an old envelope in his hip pocket. That was also the time when he performed personally every business detail from the purchase of postage stamps to the granting of credit. Now that those days were gone, he simply could not accept the fact that he possessed only finite capacity and abilities and was therefore forced to rely on others to supply needed facts and make many decisions. Sometimes he felt downright inadequate, helpless, and remote from it all. Were it not for two or three good, longtime employees whom he trusted implicitly, Eddie would have just as soon gone back to the roadside store.

Credit was the name of the game at Valley. "Terms to fit your needs" was no empty, come-on sales pitch. For only the most unworthy credit risk could some kind of a deal not be worked out, and since Valley carried its own time-payment contracts, there were no outside parties to impose restrictions on terms and conditions of the financing documents. Since the interest rates charged were the highest permitted by law—a fact that Valley did *not* advertise—and since an aggressive collection policy minimized losses, the profit that Valley earned on its credit financing often exceeded its profit from the sale of merchandise. Not bad, not bad!

It was four or five years back that Eddie Epstein finally and reluctantly came to the conclusion that he could no longer handle personally all of the details of credit granting. With the growth of all the other management problems requiring his attention, he was unavoidably neglecting this vital operation, and it was costing him money. When he at last faced up to a decision, he already had in mind the man he wanted for credit manager, one of his oldest employees and best salesman, Walter Weaver.

A few years before, when Eddie had incorporated his business, there had been a rumor among his older employees that they would be permitted to purchase stock in the new company on very favorable terms or might even be given some stock as a bonus. Though he had done nothing to give credence to the rumor, Eddie was aware of it but took no affirmative action to dispel it. Personally, he would have had no objection to such an arrangement but, on the advice of his attorney, had dismissed the idea and let the rumor die a natural death. Only Walter Weaver had ever mentioned his disappointment to his employer. Eddie had always felt a bit guilty since then.

It came as a total surprise to Weaver when the position was first offered to him. Somehow he felt that he had lost his employer's confidence, and besides he had not the foggiest notion of what credit granting involved.

"Don't worry, my boy," Eddie had reassured him. "I learned about it the hard way, and you can too. You are just as smart as I am, and we will work together until you get the hang of it."

So Walter Weaver was officially installed as credit manager, and the troops duly notified.

A few months later, Weaver came to Eddie and told him that he wanted to make a change in established procedure.

"I'm having a lot of trouble with the way the salesclerks make out the time-payment contracts," he explained. "They make a lot of mistakes, and I have to do most of them over. Also, I can't go along with some of the deals they make, and the contracts have to be changed. Why not have them bring the customer to my office, and I will make out the contract? It would save time all around."

Eddie was familiar with the problem, and as the offered solution seemed reasonable, he agreed to give it a try. Apparently it worked, for the procedure remained unchanged over the years to the satisfaction of all concerned.

Victor Velasquez, accompanied by a very troubled Chicano woman, approached the open door of Eddie Epstein's private office.

"Can I come in, Mr. Epstein? We have a problem."

He introduced his companion as Mrs. Hernandez and explained that she spoke very little English. He laid a copy of one of the store's time-payment contracts in front of Epstein.

"Last week I sold Mrs. Hernandez a new refrigerator to be delivered tomorrow. At the time, she asked me if she could make a $60 down payment—if that would be enough. I told her I was sure that that would be enough, and she showed me three $20 bills. Then I took her to Mr. Weaver's office and explained the deal to him. He said the deal was O.K. and that he would write up the contract, so I went on back to work. Yesterday, Mr. Hernandez was hurt on the job and will be laid up for a couple of months, so Mrs. Hernandez came in this morning to see if she could cancel the contract and get her $60 back. I told her to see Mr. Weaver, and I was sure there wouldn't be any problem." He paused.

"Now, she comes back to me and says that Mr.

Weaver says that she never gave him $60—that I had said there would be a $60 trade-in allowance on her old refrigerator—and that's the way he made out the contract."

Epstein inspected the document before him. It showed clearly that no cash had been paid and that only a trade-in allowance of $60 had been credited against the purchase price.

"Did you talk to Mr. Weaver?" he asked.

"Yes, I did, and do you know what? He accused me of being in cahoots with Mrs. Hernandez in trying to gyp the store out of a lousy 60 bucks!" Velasquez was livid. "I nearly punched him in the face!"

Epstein turned to Mrs. Hernandez and, calling upon his very rusty Spanish, began to question her. To each of his queries, she responded quickly and forcefully and at the end exclaimed, *"Es verdad!"* and crossed herself.

Punching an intercom button, Eddie Epstein called the store cashier.

"Linda? Vic Velasquez is bringing a Mrs. Hernandez to the office. Make out a paid-out voucher for $60, have her sign it, and give her the money. Then, just before you go to lunch come by my office, and I will tell you how to handle it on the records."

When a grateful and beaming Mrs. Hernandez had departed with Victor, Eddie closed his office door and again punched an intercom button for his warehouse foreman, Davis Doyle.

"Dave? How are we handling our trade-in appliances now? Do they all come into the warehouse like always?"

"No, Eddie, that's been changed. You remember when you were handling things you always sent the pick-up order out with the delivery order and we brought everything into the warehouse. The appliances that were worth it we fixed up and put down in the bargain basement. Some of the rest of the stuff we gave to the Salvation Army. We salvaged parts from some, and what was left we sent to the county dump. Then after Walt Weaver took over and began to issue the pick-up orders, we stopped bringing in a lot of stuff that would just have gone to the dump anyway. I guess it probably saves us some time and money. We don't pick up half of what we used to from some of our customers."

"Thanks, Dave. I just wanted to know."

The next morning Victor Velasquez was waiting for Epstein when he came in.

"Mr. Epstein. That rumble we had yesterday about Mrs. Hernandez sure shook me up. I didn't sleep much last night. You believe that we were telling you the truth, don't you?"

"Sure I do, Vic. It was just one of those things that can happen. I don't blame anybody, so just forget it."

"Thanks! I feel better, but there is something else that I thought of in the middle of the night. A few months ago, one of our other customers, Mrs. Guadalupe Garcia, told me that Mr. Weaver made the same kind of mistake on her contract. When she showed it to him a few days later, he just laughed and said he guessed he needed new glasses. Then he took her copy of the contract and scratched out the figure on the trade-in line and wrote it in on the cash-paid line, and thanked her for telling him about it. Maybe it doesn't mean anything, but I thought I ought to tell you about it."

"Thanks, Vic. I do appreciate your telling me. Now, let's just forget the whole thing and get back to work."

As the door closed, Eddie Epstein called his accounts

receivable bookkeeper and asked her to bring him Guadalupe Garcia's file.

A week later Walter Weaver strolled casually into Epstein's office and, uninvited, seated himself before the desk.

"Oh, I just came up for air. Been so busy the last few weeks, I've hardly had a chance to say hello to you. What's new, Eddie?"

"Nothing much, Walt. I manage to keep busy, too."

"I see the auditors are working in the office. A little early in the year, isn't it?"

"No, not really. I'm thinking about changing my fiscal year if it doesn't cost me too much in taxes."

"Oh."

The relief in Weaver's voice was not well concealed.

GREAT TRANSCONTINENTAL AND INTEROCEAN FIRE AND FIDELITY COMPANY

Report of Loss
Fidelity Department

ASSURED: Valley Furniture and Appliance (a corporation)
San Poco, Calizona.

RISK: Blanket fidelity bond on executive, office, and sales personnel in the principal sum of $20,000 each.

SUBJECT: Walter Webster Weaver, age 41.
211 Grande Vista, San Poco, Calizona.
Married 20 years to Wilma Weaver, age 42. One son, Walter Jr., age 19.

Employed by assured past 11 years.
No prior record of breach of fidelity.

LOSS: $28,310.

VERIFIED: By assured's regular auditors, Hutton & Button C.P.A.'s. Findings reviewed and approved by our regional audit staff.

METHOD: Subject was credit manager for assured. As such, he had assumed responsibility for preparation of all time-payment sales contracts. Many of assured's customers are Spanish-speaking people, some able to speak or read very little English. Many deal only in cash and usually make down payments in cash. When conditions were appropriate, such as the absence of witnesses, subject would, "by mistake," enter amount of cash paid as being a trade-in allowance on the contract. He would then pocket the cash.

Since subject also issued orders to pick up trade-in merchandise, no other employee would be concerned if such orders were not issued. It was also assured's accounting policy to treat trade-in allowances as discounts allowed, and the infrequent sales of trade-in appliances were treated as salvage sales. Therefore, there was no internal control to prevent or intercept a scheme such as subject had devised.

RESTITUTION: Subject and spouse have executed
                conveyance of:
                1. Residence, equity esti-
                   mated at $ 11,750
                2. Automobile, equity
                   estimated at   650
                3. Two life insurance
                   policies with surrender
                   value totaling   3,200
                              Total recovery $ 15,600

PROSECUTION: Subject pleaded guilty to three counts
                of grand theft. Sentenced to two to
                five years in state penitentiary, with
                sentence suspended on condition that
                subject serve six months in local jail
                and remain on probation for five years
                or until full restitution is made, which-
                ever is longer.

11

THE STRAWBERRY BLONDE

GLORIA Gallagher was quite a gal in her day, and in its day, Kingman's Emporium was quite a store. Like vine and tree, their daily existence was inseparably intertwined and had been for many years. When people spoke of one, the image of the other was usually in the peripheral area of concept, like crackers and cheese or bread and butter.

Kingman's Emporium, more often referred to simply as *the* Emporium, was the Macy's and Neiman-Marcus of Tuttlesville. It carried, though on a more modest scale, almost every item found in those illustrious establishments and quite a few things that they had never even heard of. Sprawling over major parts of three city blocks, the Emporium offered its customers everything from groceries to horse liniment. Its slogan—"If we haven't got it, we'll get it for you"—was a promise, a warranty, and a guarantee.

Five of its 14 major departments were housed in the main store: groceries, meat, dry goods, clothing, and hardware, together with the business office, where a dozen clerks, cashiers, and bookkeepers dealt with the daily influx of paperwork generated by a thriving and growing enterprise.

When young Kirby Kingman got off the train in the late 1880s, Tuttlesville was little more than a whistle-stop in the midst of a vast plain of dry and forbidding grassland feeling for the first time the blade of the sod-breaking plow. Were it not for the slowly advancing arteries of irrigation canals spreading from the foothills and the ensuing greening of the countryside, there was surely nothing in the environs of the village to evoke any great optimism for its future. Yet, to young Kingman, as he stood in the blazing sun on the depot platform, it looked good. It was certainly warm and it was certainly dry, and that was exactly the prescription handed to him by his doctor in Boston a month before.

It is a shame to spoil a good story. Kirby Kingman *should* have landed in Tuttlesville without two thin dimes to rub together in his pocket. He *should* have had to wash dishes or blister his soft hands digging ditches to lay the traditional foundation for establishing a successful business enterprise. The truth of the matter is that he was fairly well heeled when he began to cast about for a commercial opportunity and ended up purchasing from a discouraged and underfinanced proprietor the town's only general store. He gave the enterprise a grandiose new name, "Kingman's Emporium."

World War I had come and gone, and there was "a chicken in every pot," when Kirby Kingman finally turned the business over to his son, Kent. For 40 years the Emporium had been his very life, and he had been the very life of the Emporium. He had prudently reinvested its substantial earnings in continuous expansion and improvement, strictly on its own working capital and strictly in its own debt-free premises. It had never been necessary for Kingman to bow to the bankers—the bankers bowed to Kingman.

Young Kent Kingman held fondly to the illusion that, as a businessman, he was cast in his father's image. After two years of unspectacular attendance at State University, he had returned to Tuttlesville "to learn the business," a process still slowly in progress 15 years later. With virtually no capacity for the conception of an original idea, or the initiative to carry it out, young Kingman was content to follow precisely in his father's footsteps, and his father was content to let him do so. If privately Kirby Kingman ever felt any misgivings as to his son's real abilities, he was too proud a man to reveal them.

So, at the close of business on Monday, September 30, 1929, the senior Kingman handed the keys to his private office over to his son, and on the following Saturday sailed from San Francisco with his wife on a voyage around the world. Three weeks later, Kirby Kingman expired peacefully in his berth at sea, and on the following day, the stock market crashed in New York. (There was no connection between the two events.)

The graduation of the Tuttlesville High School class

of 1930 was a somewhat subdued and sober event. Not all the girls on the stage were bedecked in gay new dresses, and in the audience there were many solemn faces of worried parents. The future that should have been beckoning enticingly to these bright young people was greeting them instead with a dark, forbidding frown.

If there was any doubt or anxiety in the heart of Gloria Gallagher, her pixie Irish face did not show it. Sitting primly among her classmates, the overhead lights gleaming on her red gold thatch, Gloria looked confidently out into the audience, bright eyed and firm chinned. Financial adversity was no stranger to her. For three years, she had been a part-time mother to four younger sisters as their mother toiled long hours as a domestic day worker. Since her brakeman husband's fatal misstep, Grace Gallagher's life had been one of sorrow and misery, her very existence sustained only by the daily Mass and the generous credit of Kingman's Emporium. Now, Gloria was ready and eager to share the burden.

Kent Kingman was troubled. He knew with certainty that he should not be considering the hiring of another office worker. He could not delude himself any longer. Business was definitely off, and collections were progressively worsening. It would be the height of stupidity to be hiring when he should have been firing. Yet, knowing the desperate straits of the Gallagher family, and faced by those warm gray eyes, he could only ask, "Can you come to work tomorrow?"

Old Kirby Kingman had prided himself on being an upcoming and progressive businessman; indeed, for the most part the Emporium had kept pace with progress. The two outmoded objects to which he had stubbornly clung, however, were the cheap, old-fashioned sales books used in every department and the overhead trolley wires in the main store along which clerks dispatched fluttering sales tickets and currency and awaited the cashier's return of their change in the little cup.

The sales books were standard, with white and yellow tear-out copies and a tissue copy that permanently remained in the book. The Emporium bought them by the hundred gross, and if Kirby Kingman could save 10 cents a gross, he considered that he had made a major business coup.

When the new Emporium was built in 1906, the taut, shiny wires of the trolley system fanned out from the cashier's cage and across the store like a silver spider web. Small boys watched in open-mouthed fascination as the carrier cups whizzed back and forth overhead; from the window in his private office, Kirby Kingman himself would often pause, with no less avidity, to watch the inflow of currency along the wires. He was perfectly willing to buy cash registers for the outlying departments as they were opened, but in the main store he would never consider giving up the shuttling trolleys.

No one begrudged Gloria Gallagher her first assignment. No one else wanted the tedious task of sorting and alphabetizing the many hundreds of charge sales tickets that flowed daily into the office—shuffle, shuffle, shuffle all day long. While others despised the job, Gloria ate it up. Her sharp eyes and nimble fingers could finish the chore in half the time that others had done it, and then she was asking for something else to do. This course of conduct did not endear Gloria to her fellow workers, but Gloria couldn't care less. To fill her time, Mr. Kingman had extended her duties to assisting as relief cashier, had praised her work, and had secretly given her a small raise. Gloria felt smug and satisfied.

Ten years, almost to the day, after his father had

turned over the business to him, Kent Kingman did something his father had never done—he approached the bank for a loan. Those ten years of appalling depression had been brutal centuries for Kent as he had struggled desperately to keep open the doors of the Emporium. Of bitter necessity he had fired long and devoted employees and had foreclosed on old and loyal customers. At the same time, he had purposely made no record of the thousands of dollars worth of hopelessly uncollectable accounts that he had burned in the basement furnace. On paper, the assets of the Emporium still looked good. Even at depression values, their clear worth was well into the second million, but, for liquidity, the enterprise was dry as a bone and suffering from acute financial anemia.

Those years had been rough on Gloria, too. As head cashier, she sat day after day behind her wicket and with grace, kindness, and sympathy took the brunt of the abuse as desperate customers pleaded for additional credit, threatened violence, or broke down in heartrending sobs. To the limits of her endurance, she did her best to shield her employer from these added bitter blows, and while he was grateful for her loyalty and protection, he could not, of necessity, financially reward her devotion.

Gloria's life outside the store also had its problems. At worried husbands' insistence, housewives all over town had cut back on their domestic help, and Grace Gallagher had lost her last steady employment. Meanwhile, four blossoming colleens were passing into their teens and thoughtlessly making demands for more and more. It was to their sister Gloria that they turned for satisfaction and were never denied. Somehow Gloria could always manage.

Gloria was no beauty. Her freckles, snub nose, funny little mouth, and unruly strawberry blonde hair did not combine to produce a classic portrait. Nor was her stocky figure being improved by long hours sitting on a stool in a cashier's cage. It was a pair of warm gray eyes and a quick smile that balanced out Gloria's personality and together with a sharp and often salty wit made her popular with customers and friends. Though she was courted from time to time by earnest suitors, marriage was never given serious consideration as opposed to her self-perceived duties to her family.

Though Grace Gallagher daily thanked the Holy Mother for the precious gift of her daughter's filial devotion, she also included a fervent prayer for the salvation of her willful soul. Seldom at Mass, never at Confession, and often out until the wee small hours, Gloria pursued a social life that was of increasing concern to her mother. She was aware of the daily strain under which her daughter labored and the necessity for relaxation and diversion, but when Gloria began to breakfast solely on a couple of cups of black coffee and depart for work unsteady and bleary eyed, Mrs. Gallagher could only increase the frequency and fervor of her pleas for divine intercession.

Then it was 1949.

A depression had ended, and a war had been won. Business was flourishing, and debts were being paid off. The Emporium was still in business. Though the cash-carrying trolleys had been replaced by cash registers and a new bookkeeping machine installed in the office, Kent Kingman was cautious and indecisive about further changes in the pattern of operations so successfully employed by his father and so deeply ingrained in his own instincts. He was, of course, aware of the grand openings, one by one, of the new chain stores that competed directly with each department of the Emporium; but in the presence of a robust and growing economy, he felt that long-established customer loyalty, good personal service, and modest price concessions would still assure the Emporium of reaping its fair share of the business. As he had many times over the past 20 years, he wished that he could commune with the spirit of old Kirby Kingman.

Though the trolley cups no longer thudded down into the cashier's cage demanding instant attention, the still sizable flow of charge sales tickets (from the same cheap sales books) had to be processed daily, and thrifty customers still came to the store to pay their bills in cash. Gloria was not as speedy as she used to be; so when she was not as busy as she used to be, she felt quite comfortable and contented with her little world inside the cage. Her once carrot-colored hair was now a dusty dun, and her younger and less respectful associates referred privately to her as "Old Strawberry Roan." She now moved from the stool upon which she had perched for years only under press of great necessity, such as frequent trips to the women's room for a sustaining swig from the bottle that she kept in her locker. At home the younger girls had long since married and gone to establish their own rapidly growing families, and Gloria's day was often brightened by visits from one or more of her sisters proudly displaying the latest new nephew or niece who would be ceremoniously passed through the wicket to drool on her blouse or dampen her skirt. Given the chance, she would have spoiled all of them rotten.

Sherman Sullivan was a sharp young man. Aspiring to

become a C.P.A., he had accepted as a useful stepping-stone the position of office manager and head bookkeeper at the Emporium; he soon learned that any ideas he might have for upgrading accounting or fiscal procedures faced a grim gauntlet in the persons of Kent Kingman and Gloria Gallagher. Sometimes he wondered just who was actually the office manager and who was actually running the Emporium.

Until that dark day a decade past when Kent Kingman had gone, hat in hand, to put the store in hock to the local bank, no outside accountant had ever set foot in the office. Both Kirby Kingman and his son in turn had considered their own sketchy knowledge of accounting principles and procedures as being sufficient for all the needs of the enterprise. It was, therefore, an additional blow to his pride when the bank had directed Kingman, as a condition for procuring a loan, to secure an audit by independent outside accountants. Over the ensuing years, he had fussed and fumed at the nuisance and expense of the mandated annual audit, had stubbornly resisted any helpful suggestions offered for improvement, and had grimly replaced auditor after auditor who had declined a return engagement.

The repetition, however, had had its effect. The receipt of the same suggestions and the same criticisms year upon year from different impartial sources, together with a growing realization that the Emporium was no longer getting its share of the business, had forced Kent Kingman to reflect seriously upon the wisdom of persistent resistance to change. When a young local accountant, Frank Farrell, had expressed his opinions and suggestions in more conciliatory terms and had agreed to perform the audit a second year, Kent had authorized him to work with Sherman Sullivan in preparing a proposal for revision of the accounting system and of procedures for handling the fiscal affairs of the business.

As could be expected, Gloria Gallagher was not pleased that such a decision had been made without consulting her.

Frank Farrell and Sherman Sullivan sat in the latter's office with the door closed. Frank was curious.

"Sully, how long has Gloria worked here?"

Sullivan replied, "As far as I know, about 20 years. She's been here longer than anyone else in the office, and almost as long as anyone in the store. I understand that this is the only job she has ever had."

"How long has she been sorting the charge sales tickets?"

"Gosh, I don't know. My guess is that she has always done them."

"What happens to the tickets after they are posted to the customers' accounts?"

"Each day's tickets are tied in a bundle and put in a carton with the used sales books, and when the carton is full, it goes up to the attic. You should see that attic! It's got tons and tons of old records going clear back to the Year One."

"Is any reconciliation ever made of the total charges in the sales books with the total charges posted to customers' accounts?"

"No, there isn't, and there ought to be. Apparently, they have never had any such procedure. I mentioned it to Mr. Kingman once, but he said that they had never done it and he thought it was unnecessary, so I dropped it."

The two men sat silently for a few moments; then Farrell spoke.

"Sully, this is *strictly* between the two of us, but I've got a gut feeling that Gloria has something going for herself. I know she doesn't like auditors, period, and she doesn't like me in particular, but it's more than that—I think she's *afraid* of me. She's generally a pretty cool cookie, but when I come up behind her to ask her something, she nearly falls off her stool—and the back of her neck gets real red! I generally don't affect women that way, but I sure throw Gloria into a tizzy, and I'm sure it isn't just my sex appeal!" He chuckled. "I started to ask Mr. Kingman some questions about her one day, and he cut me off real short; said if I had any ideas about Gloria doing anything wrong to forget it and pack up and go home; said he felt like she was almost a daughter to him and that he would trust her with his last dollar."

Sullivan nodded.

"Yeah, he's that way about her all right. The more I think about it, the more I think you may have something. What do you want to do?"

"Well, Sully. I've got a proposition for you. How about the two of us spending a few evenings up in the attic trying to see if we can find where the body is buried—strictly on the QT, you understand."

"Sounds good to me, Frank. Count me in."

Three weeks (a hundred dusty man-hours) later, the two conspirators sat in the office of Kent Kingman, who regarded them with suspicion. He had noted Farrell's bulging briefcase and the large carton that Sullivan had brought in.

"Well," he asked irritably. "What's this all about?"

"Mr. Kingman," Farrell began. "Sully and I have been working every night and Sunday for the past three weeks up in the attic going over old records—just a minute, please!—let me finish. We were looking for something, and we found it. I am sorry to have to tell you this, but Gloria Gallagher has been stealing from you—for years."

"Ridiculous!" Kingman exclaimed. "Young man, that's a pretty serious charge, and you'd better be able to prove it! She's been audited every year, and she's never been a penny short in her accounts. Now you come along and tell me she's been stealing. Baloney! How could that be? How could she do it?"

"R-e-a-l easy. Every day she handles all the charge sale tickets. All she has to do is destroy tickets for herself and her family. That's just as good as taking cash from the safe, and that's just the way she has been doing it—for a long, long time."

Kingman's face was long and solemn, filled with disbelief.

"Go ahead," he said wearily. "How did you find out? How much has she gotten away with?"

Farrell laid a thick file of working papers on the desk.

"We went through every sales book that has been used during the past year and checked every purchase that was made by Gloria or her four sisters' families back against their customer accounts. More than half of the charges made were never posted to their accounts, and the posting copies of the sales tickets are missing also."

He opened the file, turned it toward Kingman, and flipped through page after page of long columns of figures. Kingman grunted.

"Go on, go on! How much?"

"For the past year, the total is just over $4,400— between $350 and $450 every month. When we had finished one full year, we went back farther and spot-checked six more years. In every year, we found the same pattern. There's no telling when she started or how much she has taken all together. We would have to do a detailed audit for every year to find out."

Kingman sat stunned and shaken.

"I suppose there is no way anyone else could have destroyed the tickets?"

"Not likely," countered Farrell. "Who would have profited from doing that? Gloria is the only one in the office who receives the tickets from the departments and processes them. Only the machine bookkeeper handles them after they leave Gloria; if she had wanted to destroy any tickets, she would have destroyed her own. We checked her out, too, and she's clean."

Kingman sighed.

"What do you think I should do?"

"Well, she's bonded. Perhaps you should call the bonding company."

"No, no! I can't do that to her. They would want to prosecute. After all these years, I can't do that to her. There'd be an awful stink around town. I guess I'll just have to let her go and take my licking."

A month later Sherman Sullivan stuck his head into Kent Kingman's office.

"I hear Gloria is working for Chuck Crosby."

(Crosby Hardware and Implement Company was the Emporium's oldest and bitterest competitor.)

"Humph!" grunted Kingman. "They deserve each other!"

12

PAVED
WITH GOOD (?)
INTENTIONS

Frank Flannigan knew the road-building business. He
ought to have. Over a period of 20 years, he had
worked for half of the grading and paving contractors in
the 11 western states—or so it seemed to hear him talk.
From cat-skinner to superintendent, he had served his
apprenticeship well, and he was good—he admitted it.

With easy familiarity he would rattle off the names of
dozens of prominent construction contractors for whom
he had worked, with the not-too-well-concealed inference that they were probably struggling desperately to
get along without him. His well-worn boots, his battered

old Stetson, his sunburned face with the half-chewed cigar clamped in his jowly cheeks, and his beer-barrel belly overhanging a massive belt buckle bespoke a hard-driving, hard-working, and hard-living man of the world of asphalt, gravel, and concrete.

The Holladay Construction Company was pretty much a one-man show. Harry Holladay had never been bitten by the bigger-is-better bug. He had always been content to do one good road job at a time, watching his costs, keeping up his equipment, earning a reputation for good workmanship, and also earning a comfortable profit from his effort and investment.

The office, shop, and service yard of Holladay Construction Company covered several acres; during the slack season when all of the giant tractors, graders, and trucks were brought in for cleanup and repair, the aggregate investment assembled on the premises represented well over a million dollars—all of it Harry's own hard-earned money. The well-equipped shop, efficient and orderly, was housed in a large metal building near the rear of the property; at the front stood the cinder-block structure housing the office—the nerve center of the Holladay operation.

George Gibson was grateful for his job. He had aspired to become a civil engineer, but a teenage bout with polio had left him with a shriveled arm and a short leg, and he had had to settle for a less strenuous life. When his brother-in-law, Harry Holladay, had offered him a position as payroll clerk, he was quick to accept. Now, 15 years later, he was office manager-estimator and general factotum for the organization.

It was the middle of July when it happened. The new job, 140 miles upstate, was going well—right on schedule timewise and right on target costwise. When Harry was home over the weekend, he was jubilant and optimistic. Things couldn't be better.

Then, on Tuesday afternoon, the phone rang at the office. Harry was in the intensive-care unit of a local hospital. The doctors were working on him, but they couldn't yet tell whether it was heatstroke or a cardiac problem. They thought that Mrs. Holladay should come at once, and Mr. Holladay had asked that Mr. Gibson come, also. That's all the caller could tell them.

Three hours later, George Gibson and his sister, Helen, stood tight-lipped and solemn beside Harry's bed, conscious of, but trying not to look at, the oxygen tube in his nose, the many wires running under the sheet, and the dials, monitors, and blinking lights that surrounded him. Harry smiled wanly, and his tongue was thick.

"Guess I had a close squeak. . . . Doc says I'll be laid up quite awhile. . . . Says don't worry about the job. . . . That's a laugh! Say, there was a guy in to see me Saturday. Frank something or other, Irish name. . . . Staying at the Three Star Motel. . . . Made a note on the pad on my desk. . . . He's an old road-construction man. . . . Get ahold of him and see if he will take over running the job. . . . Boy, I sure pooped out. . . ." His voice trailed off. Their five minutes up, Helen kissed him, and she and George quietly left the room.

The sales manager of Calizona Petroleum Company was furious. The telephone line almost crackled.

"I know you can't do anything about it, George. I just wish I could talk to Harry. After all these years we've done business, it hurts! We've never even had a contract— we've always given you the very best road oil price possible, and now this guy Flannigan tells us he has made other arrangements. Who the hell does he think he is?"

"I know, I know, Jack," said Gibson softly. "And I can't talk to Harry about it, either—doctor's strict orders. Harry said to put Flannigan in full charge of the job, and that's all I can do. All I know is that he sent down word that he had a better price from Mid-Cal-Pet and was going to buy from them. Guess you'll just have to wait until Harry's back on his feet and then talk it out with him."

The time cards came down on Wednesday night. On Thursday, Helen and George worked up the payroll; the paychecks went back to the job that evening for distribution to the men on Friday.

It was nearing the end of August, and the weekly payroll had been finished. Helen was working up the monthly payroll summary.

"George," she said. "It seems to me that Frank is using a lot more labor on the job than Harry did. Since they started paving, the crew has been running 30 to 35 men a week. I looked back on the last job we did, and Harry was using 25 to 30 when he was paving."

George replied, "Yeah, I know. I called Frank about it, and he said he was having a lot of trouble with the men the union sent out. A few are good men, but a lot of them are winos and bums—work a few days and then they don't show up until payday. The payroll is running a little heavy, I know. Maybe Frank doesn't get the work out of the men that Harry did. Can't tell. Since Harry took sick, I've gotten way behind on my job-cost records."

An October full moon shone down on the service yard of Holladay Construction Company and the five cars parked outside the brightly lighted office.

The cars belonged respectively to:

1. George Gibson.
2. Fred Fredricksen, Holladay's attorney.
3. Joe Jarvis, Holladay's accountant.
4. Eddie Edwards, foreman of the company's asphalt plant at the job. (He had told Frank Flannigan that now that the paving was finished he was going to take a couple of days off.)
5. The County of Jefferson, assigned to the district attorney's office, driven by Rick Richardson, assistant district attorney, accompanied by Stanley "Soapy" Smith, district attorney's investigator.

Five of the named gentlemen sat listening to Eddie Edwards.

"Hell, no!" he exclaimed, shaking a sheaf of invoices issued by Mid-Cal-Pet for delivery of road asphalt.

"If I had used that much oil, the hot mix would-a come out like soup! I never did see the delivery tags or the weight tickets on the loads—the driver always said Frank had signed for it and had kept the tags and tickets. There's one thing I'm *damned* sure of—we didn't use any more oil than we always do!"

Richardson reached for the invoices and flipped through them.

"From the looks of these, it doesn't seem to be much of an outfit. I never heard of it."

He turned to Smith.

"Soapy, I'll get out a search warrant the first thing in the morning, and you get down there and shake that place down good. Find out the name and location of the public scales that issued those weight tickets, and phone me. I'll get a warrant for it, too."

Turning to George Gibson, Richardson asked, "Did you say you thought he might take off?"

PAVED WITH GOOD (?) INTENTIONS

George nodded.

"Well, he said a few days ago that as long as just the grading of the shoulders was needed to finish the job, he might as well get ready to pull out. He said something about having a sister in Denver."

Richardson turned to Jarvis.

"Now, what about those payroll checks?"

Jarvis handed him a small package.

"There are 21 of them, made out to 13 different payees. They all appear to have been endorsed and cashed by the same person. The union says that no one with any of those names was ever sent out to the job."

Fred Fredricksen asked, "How much did you say the total was?"

"Just over $4,600," Jarvis replied. "But there are three checks still outstanding. George is going to try to stop payment on them in the morning."

Richardson spoke again to his investigator.

"You'd better check out that beer joint where these checks were cashed as soon as you can."

Frank Flannigan was thirsty. It had been two days since he had had a beer. Unfortunately, he would have to wait—the Jefferson County sheriff did not serve beer to his guests.

Nor did it help Frank's thirst and wounded ego to know that a neighboring cell confined the president, general manager, and sole proprietor of Mid-Cal-Pet, who was sadly reflecting that if only he had the $6,200 he had split with his buddy, Frank, he might have been able to make bail.

Convinced that the luck of the Irish had finally deserted him, Flannigan pleaded guilty to two counts of

101

grand theft and one count of conspiracy to defraud. He was sentenced to three to five years in the state penitentiary.

His old friend, alias Mid-Cal-Pet, likewise pleaded guilty to one count of grand theft and one count of conspiracy to defraud. For this, he drew a two-to-three-year sentence, also in the state penitentiary.

The public weighmaster got off with 90 days of local time for issuing false weight tickets.

That wrapped up the case.

The turkey smelled scrumptious. The cranberry sauce was chilled, the oyster dressing was ready to serve, and Helen had plenty of help in the kitchen. Harry Holladay, George Gibson, and Tom Traver, Harry's insurance agent and long-time fishing buddy, sat, relaxed and ready, savoring the last drop of their predinner highballs. For Harry, it was a big event—the first drink he'd had in four months.

"I've a lot to be thankful for," Harry mused. "The Man Upstairs has certainly been looking after me this year. For awhile, I thought I was a goner, but I guess He wasn't ready for me yet. And to top it all off, Tom, how can I ever thank you for twisting my arm last spring to bond my employees? You're a real pal!"

Part III

THE DEFENSIVE POSTURE

13

ON THE ALERT

Every embezzlement is definitely a custom-made, one-of-a-kind production. Every embezzlement, every embezzler, and every embezzlement opportunity is different.

As a result, there is no wide-spectrum vaccine with which the business can be inoculated against the plague of employee dishonesty. The sole defense lies in the vigilant maintenance of a perpetual physical fitness within the business body that will discourage attack and quickly disclose infection.

The first step in building the necessary defensive

posture is for the employer to reach a full realization—
reluctantly and perhaps even bitterly—that his employees
are human beings who may have the same faults and
weaknesses as those we have been reading about.
Additionally, he must become firmly convinced that the
mathematical odds that have been quoted apply inexor-
ably to *his* business. Unless he has staffed his organization exclusively with den mothers and Presbyterian
deacons, he cannot beat those odds, and unfortunately,
even such selective hiring would not reduce his risk to
zero.

There is no need, however, for the employer who has
finally opened his eyes to the sobering facts of employee
dishonesty to harbor unwarranted suspicion and distrust
of every employee and every employee motive. Such an
attitude will destroy his organization faster than plague.
Even the once-burned employer who vows never to trust
anyone again comes eventually to the inescapable
conclusion that trust and confidence are indispensable
ingredients in every successful business relationship.
Without trust, business would cease.

Rational persons, for example, come to live comfortably with a recognition of the inevitability of death and do
not allow that prospect to detract from a happy and useful
life. The rational employer will adopt the same serenity
toward the probability that his confidence someday will
be abused by a trusted employee. In both instances,
rational people exert every effort to postpone the event
for as long as possible.

Having reached a consensus with himself as to his
risk and the necessity for affirmative action, it is only
natural that the prudent employer will be properly
concerned with the cost, in terms of both effort and

money, of establishing a defensive posture. Fortunately, the initial steps are neither burdensome nor expensive. They are commonsense procedures and policies that ought to be present in every business but all too often are sadly neglected or even nonexistent. Since the cost of each subsequent step, in time and money, is generally predictable, these initial moves do not require becoming involved in a program too rich for the blood.

Nowadays, the words *communicate* and *communication* are badly overworked. (It would seem that the necessity for human dialogue had only recently been discovered.) Yet, with all we hear about its necessity, the art of communication is still sadly deficient in many areas, and one of the worst of these deficiencies is in the field of employer-employee relationships. Failure in communication is at the root of most labor strife and, in the smaller firm particularly, often the genesis of employee dishonesty.

Every organization, whether it has 5 or 500 employees, must have effective two-way communication between management and staff. Management must clearly and concisely set forth the rules of the game—"the way we do things"—so that no employee will find that he is fumbling in the dark. In turn, management must be tuned, 24 hours a day, to receive suggestions for change or improvement, as well as gripes and grievances, from employees. Should the employees of any firm come to the conclusion that management is uninterested in, or unresponsive to, their suggestions and complaints, that business is in serious trouble!

What has this to do with employee dishonesty? Simply this: Every embezzler, consciously or unconsciously, is contemptuous of his employer, resentful of his employment situation, or desirous of inflicting injury. If his decision to commit larceny needs justification in his own mind, these feelings contribute useful salve to his conscience. Perpetration of fraud would be impossible without the harboring of one or more of these attitudes. When there has been a rupture in communication, or when effective communication has never been established, the fertile soil for stealing has been prepared for planting.

The first opportunity for establishing effective communication between employer and employee arises in the hiring process. At that moment, they share a reciprocal need, one for a job and the other for a worker. This is also the moment when the employer should erect his first defense against defalcation. Even before the prospective employee is granted his first interview, he should be required to fill out a detailed employment application. With such an application before him at the time of interview, the employer can conduct his questioning in logical sequence and be assured that all pertinent points have been covered.

Regardless of a favorable first impression or an urgent need to fill a vacancy, any temptation to hire on the spot must be firmly resisted. After the interview, verification of prior employment and direct communication with personal references are vitally important steps, all too often neglected. Beware of evasive answers from former employers and fulsome praise from references; either is cause for suspicion.

If the applicant is to be hired for a position of trust or in any supervisory capacity, a full credit report from the local credit bureau might be very revealing, particularly if the individual has recently moved into the area. Inability to handle personal financial affairs will certainly cast doubt on ability to handle the employer's affairs and might well indicate a predilection to pilferage. *All too frequently, embezzlement investigations reveal that unsavory facts about the defalcator were readily available at the time of employment had proper inquiry been made.*

If two-way communication is a fact of life in the firm, the first interview is the time to disclose it. The applicant should be encouraged to ask any questions he may have about the company, working conditions, or fringe benefits. The kind of questions asked may be just as revealing of his character and attitudes as the answers secured by direct interrogation.

Such a thorough screening of potential employees admittedly is time consuming, but as the file of rejected applications grows, it will become evident that the process has saved the business from some serious mistakes. On the other side of the coin, the process has assured that the successful applicants are the best available and the most likely to contribute to the continued success of the organization.

If the expectations of both the employer and the newly hired employee are to be realized, all major conditions of the employment relationship must be understood and mutually agreeable. Should the business have more than one principal or more than a handful of employees, a clearly documented and well-circulated personnel policy is absolutely essential. For a small or medium-size enterprise, the document need not be lengthy or complex. A simple statement of policy will suffice if it covers all major areas, such as overtime, vacation and holidays, sick pay, insurance plans, and other matters of general concern and interest.

From time to time, amendment may be necessary to provide for unforseen circumstances, but basically, once adopted, personnel policy should not be tinkered with. Moreover, management must staunchly resist any temptation to deal with requested exceptions on a case-by-case basis. In only the most unusual circumstances is deviation from stated policy justified. If the situation is one likely to recur, amendment of the policy should be considered.

One of the fundamental purposes of a documented personnel policy is to assure every employee that his basic relationships, prerogatives, and privileges are identical with those of every other employee. The surest way to destroy the usefulness of the policy is to permit any appearance of favoritism or special treatment to become manifest.

The third and final step in placing the organization on the alert is the perfection of a system of internal controls. As stated in Chapter 4, "Internal controls are simply a system of *mandatory* business procedures designed to protect the assets of the enterprise and assure the accuracy of its accounting records." Note the added emphasis on the word mandatory.

There is no use being coy about the purpose of internal controls or about the strict compliance demanded of every person in the organization—including management. The assets they are designed to protect are the very lifeblood of the business, and employee theft is the bleeding ulcer that can drain away that precious fluid. Just because the firm has exerted every effort toward a liberal personnel policy and pleasant working conditions, it does not mean that it has surrendered its right to insist that its internal controls are observed and to take stern action against any employee failing to do so. The order of the day is emphatically, "Shape up or ship out!"

Because every embezzlement starts with a breach of internal controls, auditors are fully justified in taking very seriously such seemingly minor matters as a missing canceled check or a misfooted journal column. Only thorough investigation can determine whether the breach is an innocent mistake or part of a carefully planned scheme of defalcation. The reason for this concern should be understood and recognized by all involved and not attributed to nit-picking by a persnickety auditor.

The beneficial effects of adopting the basic program described will soon become evident throughout the organization. The honest and competent employees will be heartily in accord with its objectives and will extend full cooperation. They are fully aware of the necessity of well-defined policies and procedures, and they work most comfortably and efficiently when such are in effect. Hostility or resistance to new measures by any employee may well be reason to review his usefulness to the firm. There just might be an ulterior motive behind his reluctance to cooperate.

Once the shakedown period has passed, management will realize that the whole business is running more smoothly and that many of the annoying little problems of operation and personnel have been reduced or eliminated. Nagging doubts about whether all normal security measures have been put into force will be dispelled, and a wholesome new spirit may even be evident throughout the organization.

For a change, being the boss just might be fun again.

14

SHARING THE RISK

Probably the most frequently recurring statement contained in the reports of embezzlement investigations, and the saddest commentary, is: *"The suspect was not bonded."*

Whereas the average business is plastered with fire insurance, blanketed with liability insurance, and well covered against many other risks, it probably stands fully exposed against the hazard of employee dishonesty—a hazard statistically greater than fire.

In view of the size and persuasiveness of the American insurance industry, it is completely beyond understanding that a collective risk as vast as the potential for employee stealing remains so widely uninsured. Reputedly ready, willing, and able to insure every conceivable risk, the current performance of the industry in the field of fidelity insurance is absolutely pitiful.

To discover, if possible, the reasons behind this strange situation, I asked several independent general insurance agents for their opinions. All were frank and helpful, and the information they supplied was very revealing.

First, I asked the agents to estimate in terms of premiums earned the approximate ratio of their fire insurance business to their fidelity insurance business. The responses were very consistent at about 100 to 1—100 times as much fire insurance as fidelity insurance. Assuming a 50–50 distribution of fire insurance between residential and commercial risks, it appears that businesses are spending 50 times as much to insure themselves against fire loss as against fidelity loss even though "the losses to employers from embezzlement exceed those caused by fire in a substantial measure."[1]

While reasons stated for this disparity varied from agent to agent, there was a general consensus on the major points.

First, only a handful of the leading insurance companies emphasize fidelity underwriting as an important part of their business. Many general insurance companies do not write fidelity insurance at all. Some companies previously writing such coverage have dropped the line. For the majority of the companies that do provide it, fidelity insurance is offered on a basis of "if you want it, we have it"—simply as an add-on service to customers for other lines.

Agents consulted agreed that companies made little attempt to encourage agents to put more effort into writing fidelity insurance. They were generally niggardly in supplying agents with up-to-date sales literature. (One agent reported the recent receipt of a brochure originally issued by the underwriter over 15 years ago.) Instructional seminars are few and far between, and media advertising stressing fidelity insurance, essential to a vigorous sales effort, is very limited and spotty.

The agents noted that some underwriters complain of severe losses and general lack of profitability in fidelity insurance. However, in 1980 the Surety Association of America released data from a study of 12 years of industry experience, 1967 through 1978, which showed an overall loss ratio of only 55.9 percent of premiums.[2] While companies probably would not get fat on such margins, there is strong indication that with a little more effort, and particularly in view of the vast potential market, the line could be made very profitable.

Secondly, the agents readily agreed, the average agent expends little energy on the promotion of fidelity insurance. With perhaps a score of other lines to write, lines that have more public demand and less sales resistance, he concentrates on that business to the neglect of fidelity insurance. Too, as one agent expressed, in the face of rising premiums and the resulting howls of anguish from his assureds, the agent is often happy just to secure the renewal of existing coverages. No way, José, is he going to jeopardize sure business to play missionary.

It is also true that, while the insuring agreement—the bond—is very simple and brief, the wide variety of terms and options used in selecting the right coverage for each client requires of the agent a thorough knowledge of both his client's internal operations and the options in the available coverages. Since the low volume of fidelity business currently written does not encourage him to devote the study necessary to keep up to date and well informed, he may be reluctant to expose his ignorance by making a direct sales approach to his clients.

Somewhat sheepishly, a surprising number of the agents admitted that their own employees were not bonded! Yes, they had heard the First Commandment of Salesmanship: "If you don't use it, you can't sell it."

The whole posture of the insurance industry— companies and agents alike—is reminiscent of this pointed story often told at sales meetings. A shoe factory sent two of its salesmen to two of the new nations of Africa to survey the sales potential.

A few days after his arrival, one of the salesmen cabled his home office:

"SITUATION HOPELESS. NOBODY WEARS SHOES. RETURNING HOME."

A few days later, the other salesman cabled:

"FANTASTIC OPPORTUNITY. NOBODY WEARS SHOES. SEND SAMPLES."

The third and final set of reasons cited by the queried agents was an almost exact recital of the points covered in this book concerning the ignorance and indifference of the average employer:

1. Refuses to face the statistical facts of loss probability.
2. "I trust my employees." (Famous last words!)
3. Is afraid of offending employees by bonding them.

4. "Too much insurance now."
5. Doesn't understand and doesn't want to know the wide options for coverage.
6. "Can't afford it."
7. "Can't be bothered."
8. "Get lost!"

So much for the three corners of the triangle.

Now and then, however, the agent encounters a live one. After he has recovered from shock and has an application in hand, there are still some hurdles to leap before he can spend his commission. Since the sudden interest of a client in fidelity insurance is often prompted by a recent loss, the underwriting company quite naturally will want to know what steps the prospect has taken to correct the internal conditions that made the loss possible. It is not about to insure an employer who has not profited by experience.

Even if the applicant has not had a prior fidelity loss, the company will still want to know what internal controls are in effect, the frequency of external audits, and the thoroughness of prehiring investigation of new employees. Failure to employ any of these commonsense procedures makes the risk less attractive to the underwriter and may bring a "No, thank you" in response to the application.

Assuming a sincerely interested employer and a knowledgeable agent, an effective and affordable fidelity insurance program can be designed to fit the needs of every size and kind of business. Few lines of insurance are more flexible and adaptable to each individual circumstance.

A vital process in the establishment of a fidelity insurance program is a realistic, hard-nosed appraisal of the degree and amount of risk inherent in each position and with each employee. There is a regrettable tendency to underestimate the risk, consciously in an effort to cut costs or unconsciously through failure to perceive the probable size of a possible loss. Employees not directly handling money or merchandise sometimes will be deemed to present no risk at all and be excluded from coverage. A big mistake! Millions of dollars of merchandise, for example, have gone out the back door in trash cans or "empty" cartons aided or abetted by meek janitors and conspiring disposal truck drivers. Definitely, every employee should be covered. If the risk is small, the premium will be modest, also.

In a spot check of surety companies' claim files, covering retail, wholesale, manufacturing, and service-type businesses and a wide range of positions from bookkeepers to managers, the Surety Association of America discovered a widespread prevalence of under-insurance.[3] In one group of typical cases, the total embezzlement loss was $783,000, the total bond coverage $208,000, leaving an uninsured loss of $575,000,—73.5 percent of the total! For those employers, underinsurance has been a costly experience.

Though initial premiums will generally be set "by the book," periodic review and favorable experience should produce subsequent premium reductions. Interim correction of deficiencies in internal controls, utilization of professional accounting services, and adopting of effective screening of new employees will all contribute to lower costs.

While the basic purpose of fidelity insurance is to compensate for loss from employee dishonesty, valuable side effects are inherent in a bonding program. A bonded employee will think twice before he yields to temptation. He knows that if he is caught, there will be no monkey business with the bonding company and no chance to sweet-talk his way out of trouble as he might with a lenient employer.

Not infrequently does it happen that a promising applicant for employment fails to return for a second interview once he has learned that he will be bonded. Perhaps he (or she) has already been caught with sticky fingers and is looking for a new pigeon in order to play a repeat performance, or there may be some other reason why he does not wish to be scrutinized by a bonding company investigator. In such an event, the prospective employer can feel very lucky—he probably has had a narrow escape.

Employers contemplating the purchase of fidelity insurance are often apprehensive that the announcement that they are adopting a bonding program might have an unfavorable impact on employee morale. They are fearful that it might be misinterpreted as a lack of confidence and trust. They need not be. Honest employees with good intentions, worthy of positions of trust, will not be offended. They will be the first to approve, for they fully appreciate that the personal integrity of which they are proud is not universally distributed.

If the proposed program is tactfully presented to the employees simply as a normal extension of the firm's existing insurance coverage, of no more significance than an increase in public liability limits, there should be minimum adverse reaction. It is, of course, of vital importance that there be no suggestion or inference, even in jest, that the move has been prompted by any doubt or suspicion of the trustworthiness of any employee. A blunder in this respect would be most unfortunate.

No matter how smoothly the subject has been introduced to the employees, there still may be an occasional individual who will display hurt feelings or evidence resentment. Should such an attitude persist beyond a reasonable initial reaction, the employer might do well to reflect on these wise words of Shakespeare: *"The lady doth protest too much, methinks."*

NOTES

1. *Forty Thieves* (Baltimore: United States Fidelity and Guaranty Company, 1970).
2. *Twelve-Year 1967–1978 Fidelity Experience* (Iselin, N.J.: The Surety Association of America, 1980).
3. *Safeguards Against Employee Dishonesty in Business* (Iselin, N.J.: The Surety Association of America, N.D.)

15

OLD EAGLE EYE

Every accountant is well aware of the popular conception that his primary function as an auditor is to catch the guilty and scare hell out of the innocent. He is also aware of the unflattering appraisal of his anatomy and personality in the oft-cited paraphrase from the late writer Elbert Hubbard:

> The typical auditor or accountant is a man past middle age, spare, wrinkled, intelligent, cold, passive, non-committal, with eyes like a codfish, polite in contact, but at the same time unresponsive, cool,

calm, and as damnably composed as a concrete post or a plaster of paris cast; a human petrification with a heart of feldspar, and without charm or the friendly germ, minus passions and sense of humor. Happily, though, they seldom reproduce—and finally all of them go to Hell!

That this description is not too far from the image of him shared by some of his friends, clients, and much of the general public disturbs him not a bit. He knows that his penchant for precision, his tenacity in the pursuit of obscure accounting and taxation principles, and, most of all, his damnable composure and pragmatism mark him as a weirdo in the minds of many. No wonder his profession has never been selected for a Perry Mason or a Dr. Welby type of prime-time serial.

Notwithstanding such a horrendous public image, most accountants manage to bear up very well, thank you, and to attain the high esteem of their clients and an acceptable economic reward. There is not much visible evidence of any great effort on their part, either individually or as a profession, to dispel this mystique; in fact, many practitioners seem to enjoy the distinction and use it as an effective tool in their professional kit. The possibility of the unexpected appearance of an auditor can be an effective deterrent to hanky-panky between the ledger sheets.

Though they may react with blissful disregard to their rather grim public image, accountants are vitally concerned with the lag in recognition of the value of their services in assisting smaller business management with the harassing problems that seem to be snowballing in every industry and commercial activity. Few competent

*"I see money, yachts, beautiful ladies . . . now appears
gentleman with brief case labeled 'auditor' . . ."*

accountants are looking for work. Many of them already
are working some horrible hours. It is not new clients that
they seek but rather greater and more effective use of
their talents by the clients they already have. In no area is
this shortfall of utilization more costly and prevalent than
in the protection of business assets from employee
dishonesty.

In many business and industrial firms, independent
accountants are already performing annual audits for the
certification of financial statements and the preparation
of the necessary income tax returns; but, having completed these annual chores, they may not be consulted or
called upon for other services before another year has

rolled around. Because of the major importance of the financial statement and the tax returns, and the fact that the fee for these services may be substantial, the proprietor may tend to feel that he has received all the accounting services for which he has any need and may assume that the audit has also vouched for the honesty of all his employees.

If he has jumped to this latter conclusion, it is the fault of his accountant. Certainly, if the prescribed letter of engagement has been submitted by the accountant to his client, it would spell out exactly what the audit was designed to cover and what the accountant's responsibility was in that connection.[1] An audit for financial statement purposes, even if it has followed precisely the "generally accepted auditing procedures," is *not* a warranty that there is no hocus-pocus in the nether reaches of the firm's records or operating methods. True, even during routine financial statement audits, sticky-fingered culprits are sometimes uncovered, but such cases are often more of a serendipitous by-product than the result of specific investigation for that purpose.

Thirty years ago I expressed in print a doubt about whether standard auditing methods are infallible in the detection of embezzlement. This opinion is still being cited by recognized authority.[2]

First, the majority of defalcations occur in the level of business transactions not normally subjected to the auditor's detailed scrutiny.

Second, the perfect system of internal controls has never been invented and probably never will be.

Third, the versatility of embezzlers is astounding and greatly underestimated.

And finally, in my opinion, the emphasis of

auditing education and techniques has been placed on routine factual verification rather than upon analytical study and inquisitive reflection.[3]

It is this "analytical study and inquisitive reflection" that distinguishes the audit or investigation for security purposes and the capacity for such study and reflection that marks the skilled investigator. *An insatiable curiosity is the hallmark of a good auditor. Devoid of curiosity, regardless of other qualifications, he is not worth his salt.*

Ideally, a program for security audit should be designed to dig deeply into every corner of the business operation where a possibility for employee theft of money, merchandise, or other property of value exists, and the plan should be ongoing and unscheduled. The uncertainty of the timing but the certainty of eventual occurrence is the very essence of the program's effectiveness. Once all personnel become aware of such audits, sloppy procedures will be tightened up and any employee contemplating larceny will certainly pause for reflection.

A good investigative auditor works like a good bird dog, sniffing behind every clump of grass and under every bush. It is not at all farfetched to say that many times he will "smell" the scent of wrongdoing before there is any tangible evidence (see Chapter 11). Too, like the bird dog, he cannot be hurried or pushed. Analytical study and inquisitive reflection are not aided by the imposition of time limits. If the auditor is pressed for available time because of other commitments, or if the client is holding a stopwatch and continuously reckoning the cost, both the accountant's time and the client's money are being wasted and the engagement should be terminated. That is not to say that both time and money cannot be effectively budgeted; they can be to the complete satisfaction of both parties. While the exact time required to explore thoroughly any particular area cannot be determined in advance, the total time for the entire project can be agreed upon and priorities established for performance. There is no need for the client to give the accountant a blank check, and any ethical accountant capable of undertaking such a task is as anxious as his client that the expenditure will be cost effective. Fortunately, once the project is established and the first go-round has been completed, the auditor's familiarity with every facet of the operation will permit him subsequently to touch many bases with only a quick look to assure that nothing has gotten out of line since his last inspection. Thus, unless the business is expanding rapidly or new problem areas have developed, the time and expense required to maintain effective control will be substantially reduced.

From time to time the accountant will probably submit suggestions to his client for changes in procedure, reassignment of personnel, or acquisition of new equipment or facilities. The prudent accountant will go slowly in trying to bring about radical change, no matter how badly it may be needed. At the same time, the client should be prepared to give serious consideration to proposals presented and be willing to listen to valid reasons and to follow insofar as possible the advice given. After all, that is what he is paying the accountant for.

The businessman who teams up with his accountant in such a program as described will soon become aware that the benefits are many and far-reaching. Harassed as he typically is by the daily demands on his time and physical and mental energies just to keep the doors open and the bills paid, he is still keenly conscious that he is of necessity neglecting many important areas of his responsibility. After all, while he is just one man, inescapably "the buck stops here." He also realizes that the areas not receiving his close attention may be the very spots where costly employee dishonesty could take place. It is, therefore, probable that the first tangible benefit that he will perceive will be a profound sense of relief that somebody is at last covering the bases that he had been unable to attend to. Now he can sleep nights.

Certainly, there will be some grumbling and foot-dragging in the organization as successive necessary changes are put into effect. Old work patterns—and old nonwork patterns—are hard to change. Some departmental pecking orders will shift, and some noses will surely be bent. Ancient routines will be replaced and some cherished prerogatives eliminated, and the accountant's popularity may plummet to that of a skunk at a picnic. While the employer certainly must listen to and consider carefully any legitimate static, he will need to get the message to the troops, firmly and with finality, that this is the way it's going to be. Good programs are known to have been sabotaged by vacillation at the top level. In due time, the flak will stop and the employees will settle into their new routines.

As in the case of adopting a bonding program, it is absolutely essential that the employer and the accountant, both by spoken word and by attitude, never give cause for any employee to feel that he is under direct suspicion or that the honesty of the staff in general is being questioned; nor should the investigative work of the accountant have the slightest appearance of a witch hunt. Should such impressions gain general acceptance, the work of the accountant could be seriously hampered and the morale of the organization unnecessarily damaged. The soft, smooth, patient approach will do more to assure success than any show of authority or application of pressure.

In the cases of some larger clients, the business assets in need of protection may include warehouses, manufacturing or processing plants, and transportation systems. Total security involves both internal and external protection.

Though overall security is an integral part of any system of internal controls, and therefore of direct concern to the accountant, the expertise required to implement and maintain extensive physical protection is usually beyond his skills. In such cases, the services of a competent professional security agent are indispensable. When a client's business has rapidly expanded or when existing facilities are inadequately protected, the accountant should recognize this and recommend that his client employ professional security services.

Because both the accountant and the security agent are concerned with the protection of business assets, a potential exists for friction between them. Generally, the accountant's sphere of responsibility should be the oversight of the internal controls and direct concern for the safety of liquid and intangible assets, while the security agent should concern himself primarily with the protection of physical properties from both internal and external loss. In some instances, such as with inventories, fine lines of responsibility cannot be drawn or responsibility must be shared. Definite understandings must be worked out among the client, the accountant, and the security agent. Cordial, helpful cooperation by all concerned is essential and mutually beneficial.

In recent years a disturbing assumption has developed in some business and governmental circles that, because accountants have long advocated better business procedures and tighter internal controls to discourage employee dishonesty, they have by inference guaranteed the effectiveness of such measures and should be held accountable when losses still occur. What a ridiculous proposition! When have fire departments been held responsible for fires or police departments for burglaries? All that accountants have been trying to do is convince employers that embezzlement could be reduced—not eliminated—by the use of some sensible precautions of proven effectiveness.

And that is all that I am trying to do.

NOTES

1. Don E. Giacomino, "Fraud and the Auditor," *The National Public Accountant* (April, 1980), pp. 26–29.
2. Donald R. Cressey, "Management Fraud, Accounting Controls, and Criminological Theory." Paper presented at the Peat, Marwick, Mitchell Symposium on Management Fraud, Glen Cove, New York. June 1–2, 1978.
3. Wm. W. McCullough, "Embezzlement, a Rising Menace," *The California Accountant* (October 1949), pp. 7–13.

16

BITTER MEDICINE

A s already stated, I have no desire to give helpful
advice or encouragement to those readers who may
already be busily engaged in diverting their employers'
assets or who may be seriously contemplating joining up
with the increasing multitude engaging in that form of
indoor sport. The primary purpose of this book is directly
the opposite: to arouse the dormant defensive instincts
of present and potential victims of the crime of embezzlement.

Unfortunately, the soporific effects of ignorance,
inertia, and indecision have so anesthetized millions of

employers that only the most shocking statistics and brutal warnings can alert them to self-defense. It is, therefore, with great reluctance that perhaps the most unbelievable statistic of all is revealed herewith. If, in a last desperate effort to arouse the sleepers, some comfort and succor is thereby given to miscreants, it is unfortunate. The risk is, indeed, calculated. The statistic: *No felony in the index of the criminal code has less chance of resulting in penal servitude than the crime of embezzlement.*

One of the most profitable ventures in which the odds makers of Las Vegas or the Mafia of Newark could engage would be to offer "accident" insurance to practicing embezzlers (for a small fraction of the loot) that would compensate generously for hard time served. The *insurors* would make a fortune.

The reason is that between the detection of the crime and the slamming of the cell door an incredible gauntlet of obstacles, procedural difficulties, and human perversity tilts the scales of justice in favor of the criminal. According to the American Bar Association, 91 percent of those convicted of bank robbery were sentenced to prison compared with only 17 percent of those convicted of embezzlement of bank funds. Since they are generally federal crimes, offenses against banks are accorded a high priority in the criminal justice system, and it can be reasonably assumed, therefore, that even a 17 percent rate of incarceration is an optimum not to be expected in the prosecution of the mill run of embezzlers through the state courts.

In case the point has been overlooked, it is probably in order to emphasize that the numbers cited refer only to *convicted* embezzlers. Conviction, of course, must be preceded by arraignment and prosecution. At each of these three levels, there are many holes in the sieve through which the culprit may slip unscathed. While some of these holes are the often incomprehensible technicalities of our so-called system of criminal justice, the prosecution of the crime of embezzlement is surrounded by its own peculiar collection of impediments that help to account for the deplorably minute portion of trust violators who ever view the world through prison bars.

In its 1977 "Crimes Against Business" report, American Management Associations notes these problems of successful prosecution:

> Business executives report only a small proportion of known offenses to the criminal justice system, which they see as excessively time consuming and generally nonresponsive to their needs; there is, too often, little or no communication between the business and criminal justice communities.
>
> Police and prosecutors are often ill-prepared to handle crimes against business, especially the more complex kind.
>
> Crime statutes are often inadequate for effective prosecution. . . .
>
> Patterns of sentencing for crimes against business, and economic crimes in general, appear arbitrary and discriminatory.

The first and largest stumbling block in the process of bringing the disclosed defalcator to justice is the victim himself. Whereas the victims of crimes ranging from theft of the morning paper to armed robbery are quick and vocal in their demands for vengeance, the swindled employer all too often turns into a quivering softie when faced with the decision to institute prosecution. The screams of anguish that erupted at the first disclosure of his loss fade away to faint whimperings and his vows of vengeance to vacillation.

Reasons for this reaction among employers are many, varied, and often complex, but first and foremost is the fact that, as previously mentioned, employer negligence in some degree is an essential element of every embezzlement, and the sobering realization of that fact is not pleasant to the newly initiated. As his sins of omission and commission parade through his mind, he feels the egg on his face grow deeper and stickier and fears that he will stand exposed as a prize boob before his family, his associates, and his other employees. (The pilfering employee, of course, already knows that.)

Often there has been a long and otherwise happy employer-employee relationship and, of course, substantial extension of trust and confidence by the employer. There may have been pleasant socializing between families, shared triumphs and tragedies, and the daily little human contacts over the years. Suddenly, this blissful relationship is shattered in a blinding flash. The trusted one stands exposed as a common thief. Had he (or she) perished in a traffic crash or dropped dead of a heart seizure, the grief of his disillusioned victim would not have been more poignant.

The 180-degree turn required to press charges in such circumstances is often more than the distressed employer can navigate, and only strong reminders from himself and others can bring him around to fulfilling his painful obligation. It will take a rebirth of fortitude, plus perhaps the strong urging of his attorney and his accountant, and maybe some fatherly encouragement from the district attorney, before he brings himself to gulp his pride and prefer the necessary charges.

Unless and until every wronged employer is ready to disregard his personal distaste and inconvenience and willingly assist authority in pursuit of swift and certain punishment, there will be no decline in the wave of employee thievery that is eating away at the very foundations of private enterprise.

Now and then a disclosed embezzler walks away from the scene of his crime, head high and grinning like a Cheshire cat. Knowing "where the body is buried" can be potent insurance against a free vacation in the big house. Perhaps the boss has been cheating on his wife or on the Internal Revenue Service, submitting phony invoices on a cost-plus contract, or accepting kickbacks. Few people are without some human frailty that they would just as soon not have exposed to public gaze, and the compleat embezzler is quick to latch onto such juicy bits of blackmail and file them away for future use. Since wild horses and Brahma bulls cannot drag cooperation out of such a wayward victim, the frustrated prosecutor had just as well move on to his next triple ax slaying.

A somewhat unholy alliance occasionally may defeat prosecution when the employer and his bonding company smell the possibility of full or substantial restitution. Naturally, both are interested in reducing the net cash loss to a minimum, and their willingness to compromise the principle of vigorous prosecution is understandable. Perhaps the culprit has repleviable assets or affluent relatives. Doting parents, who cannot stand the thought of Little Willie (age 42) going to jail, have been known virtually to hock their Social Security check to get him out of trouble—for the umpteenth time! Money talks, and at no time does it talk more loudly than when a deal is in the making to forswear prosecution in exchange for restitution.

Fortunately, in most jurisdictions there are alternatives that can start the wheels of justice turning without requiring the employer to initiate prosecution. Given hard evidence of the crime, the district attorney may proceed on his own volition, or a grand jury may take official notice and issue an indictment. In all such cases, however, the victim will be required at least to furnish evidence and testimony; hopefully, his sense of civic duty will be strong enough to impel him to perform this minimal assistance.

Sometimes the action of the disclosed defalcator will obviate the necessity of a formal move to bring him to justice. As previously noted, a surprising number of persons accused of embezzlement will confess readily when confronted with strong evidence of their crime and, with or without counsel, throw themselves on the mercy of the court.

Every so often, however, a cool cookie, carefully calculating the odds and perhaps with the encouragement of a litigious defense attorney, will elect to go the whole route regardless of how damning the evidence may be against him. This decision, and any legal advice that prompted it, may be very sound, for sometimes the peculiarities of a complex embezzlement case can be very favorable to the defense.

All but the most simple cases generally involve accounting records, procedures, and concepts. Discovery may have been made by an accountant, the evidence largely developed by an accountant, and an accountant will probably be a principal witness for the prosecution. Herein lie some problems. Recognizing fully the pitfalls of generalizations, we can, however, state with considerable accuracy that:

1. Attorneys (including judges and prosecutors) do not understand accounting and do not like cases involving accounting.
2. Jurors dislike accounting (and accountants), and they can absorb only the most elementary accounting concepts.
3. Accountants have difficulty in communicating accounting information effectively to nonaccountants.

Nothing much can be done about juries. The average citizen has a mind-set against anything that smacks of bookkeeping, and he is not about to learn. Him, we can forgive; but it is incomprehensible that, in an age and economy in which the professions of law and accountancy so frequently serve mutual clients whose legal and accounting affairs can be inseparably intertwined, one profession should be so ignorant of the principles of the other. The spheres of law and accountancy are becoming increasingly interdependent; in order to serve common clients effectively, it is imperative that the practitioners of each profession understand the basic tenets of the other.

For many years, accounting students have been required to master the laws of commerce and taxation, but as yet few law schools require exposure of their students to even the elementary principles of accounting. Something has got to give!

Many cases of violation of financial trust involve

defendants with sophisticated knowledge of accounting and the intricacies of fiscal procedure. Defense attorneys in such cases, ably coached by their own clients, can often razzle-dazzle prosecutors and judges ill equipped to cope on an equal footing.

If the case at hand involves any degree of accounting complexity, and if his own accounting expertise is at the low norm of his profession, the wise prosecutor will bring the accountant into early association and will rely heavily on his assistance. Such teamwork in the preparation and presentation of the technical evidence in bite sizes for the jury and judge may be a crucial factor in obtaining a conviction.

Despite meticulous preparation and patient, logical presentation of the evidence, the prosecution of an embezzlement case can come a cropper on the home stretch when the jury files out to begin deliberation. Regardless of how carefully the jury may have been selected, it will probably contain one or more of those exasperating individuals who perversely cling to a belief that somehow the violation of financial trust is *different* from other crimes. They seem to think that it is not a "real" crime—that it is some kind of a parlor game played with dice and funny money. They may believe—particularly if the employer is a large concern—that employee pilfering is just another risk that the employer should grin and bear. Should the ill-gotten gains have provided the accused with some of the exotic goodies of life, even briefly, a certain amount of vicarious envy and admiration may be felt. And, in view of the tremendous odds in favor, the chance also is excellent that some juror may be soberly reflecting, "But for the Grace of God, there stand I."

and drastically reduced, and the imminent threat of
retribution reestablished in the minds of those who may
be tempted, employers had just as well unlock their safes
and cash registers, throw open their warehouse doors,
and yell, "COME AND GET IT!"

17

A TEXTBOOK CASE

I have never met Jay Robert Maisel, but I shall be eternally grateful for his unintentional assistance in completing this book. Just as I was beginning to cast around for ideas and material for the final chapter, Mr. Maisel arranged to get himself arrested for allegedly embezzling nearly $700,000 from the office of the controller of the City of Phoenix, Arizona. (Luckily, his attempt to steal another $441,000 failed.)

Though at the moment the investigation is incomplete, facts as reported to date by *The Arizona Republic* and *The Phoenix Gazette* are sufficient to establish the affair as a classic textbook case for students of the crime of embezzlement.*

According to *Republic* features writer Tom Fitzpatrick, Maisel, 37, was a habitual criminal who, during a career of over 20 years, had served time in four maximum-security prisons. His convictions included three terms for auto theft in Colorado, California, and Texas and conversion of a motor home rented in Phoenix and sold in California. He was also convicted or charged on several lesser offenses such as drug peddling, attempted rape, and assault. His crowning achievement, however, was piggy-backing his criminal career by embezzling funds from the Arizona State Prison where he was employed as a clerk while serving time.

From the foregoing, it is crystal clear that Maisel was eminently qualified for further pursuit of a life of crime, but how in Heaven's name did he make a successful connection and land a job with the controller's office in a major American city?

It seems that there is a federally funded program known as Job Stimulus designed to help ex-convicts get a fresh start. Maisel, a "client" of the program, was sent to the controller's office by a man named Oscar Douglas. Asked if he knew of Maisel's record as an embezzler, Douglas said,

"I had a good interview with Maisel. He was very frank about his being an ex-convict. But I don't recall him telling me about embezzling. If he had, I probably would have sent him to another type of job."

In the controller's office, Maisel was interviewed by Evan Francis.

*Excerpts reprinted by permission of *The Arizona Republic* and *The Phoenix Gazette*.

"I never saw his record," Francis said. "But I do recall him telling me how horrible it was in prison and how he never wanted to go back."

City Controller Gary Gross also said he knew nothing of Maisel's record as an embezzler.

"I checked with the Phoenix Police Department," Gross said. "They gave me the go-ahead. They said he was all right to hire. So I did."

(Is it fair to ask, where does innocence end and stupidity begin?)

All the while various officials were rubber-stamping Maisel's fitness for employment in a public position of trust, his complete dossier was in the public record not a city block from the controller's office. Any official who wanted to take the trouble could have uncovered the whole sorry mess in a few minutes.

Tom Fitzpatrick concludes his revealing story with this pungent goody:

> According to police investigators, Maisel embezzled the money by duplicating checks in large amounts. One was for a staggering $514,000.
> "I know it sounds like a large amount," Gross said. "But we have lots of big checks going through this office." Gross said it with a straight face.

(Internal controls? What are they?)

A few days after this first story broke, a staff writer on the *Republic,* Susan Leonard, wrote:

> Phoenix police suspect that a city employee charged with embezzling almost $700,000 also

attempted to embezzle an additional check that would have brought the total to more than $1.1 million.

The latest bogus check, written for $441,000, has been recovered, said Capt. Thomas Agnos, head of the Phoenix Police Department's general investigations bureau.

City officials originally disclosed that Jay Robert Maisel, a convicted embezzler employed in the city controller's office, was arrested Sept. 6 for investigation of defrauding the city of $697,349.

At the time, city and police officials knew that someone had arranged for a city check for $441,000 to be sent to a California address in a scheme similar to the one Maisel allegedly used to embezzle the other money, Agnos said.

However, he said, they did not disclose information about the bogus check because it was never deposited or cashed.

"The money was never in jeopardy," Agnos said. "There was never a risk that the city would lose the money because we had the city stop payment on the check."

City Controller Gary Gross said the check, dated August 22, was sent to a mail forwarding service in Hollywood. It was addressed to Planning Research, a legitimate company in Huntington Beach, Calif., that the city has done business with.

(Thank you, Susan Leonard.)

(The good police captain is entitled to his own definition of jeopardy, but in my book, when a negotiable check has been bouncing around the country for nearly two weeks during which time no one knew where it was, or even of its existence, the funds required to cover it were definitely at risk.)

Two weeks after Maisel's arrest, the City of Phoenix took official notice of the fiasco uncovered in the controller's office. Frank Turco, another *Republic* staff writer, reported:

> Disciplinary action will be taken against the supervisor who approved the hiring of an ex-convict who allegedly embezzled nearly $700,000 in city funds, Phoenix City Manager Marvin Andrews said Thursday.
>
> Andrews said some type of action will be taken against City Controller Gary Gross for using "bad judgment" in authorizing the employment in his office of Jay Robert Maisel earlier this year.
>
> Andrews said he has not decided on the extent of disciplinary action. He added that a decision will not be made until next week, after he receives recommendations from two of Gross's superiors, Selden Kent, manager of administrative services, and Alex Cordova, finance director.
>
> Andrews refused to speculate on what the action might include.
>
> "There is no doubt that he (Gross) used bad judgment," Andrews said.

In its issue of September 20, City Hall Reporter Edythe Jensen of *The Phoenix Gazette* quotes City Manager Andrews as saying that before any disciplinary action can be taken, the city must first determine "how much of this thing was the fault of the system and how much was the fault of individuals."

Andrews also reportedly blames federal privacy acts for denying his personnel officials access to arrest records, yet he and, presumably, his officers were not aware that much of the information needed to make an informed opinion on Maisel was contained in Maricopa County Superior Court records kept within a block of his office and wide open to public scrutiny.

(The Great American Alibi: It was the system—or the computer.)

An interesting sidelight is attributed to Assistant City Manager Peter F. Starrett, who said that because of federal job programs "we probably would have had to hire Maisel anyway. We are getting sued all the time for refusing to hire people for whatever reasons."

Starrett also notes that auditors are examining internal procedures in the municipal offices, and that study committees are at work on the city's hiring policies "in an effort to introduce more safeguards and prevent future embezzlements."

(Nice going, Edythe Jensen. That kind of reassurance must be comforting to the good citizens of Phoenix.)

The outcome of the Phoenix case is predictable. We need not await the reports of further developments. After the round robin of finger-pointing by city officials, and then the sketchy reports—buried on page 17-H—of Mr. Maisel's prosecution, the Phoenicians will settle back to their blissful enjoyment of desert sunshine and clean air.

As the details of the case and the indignation of the moment fade from memory, so will the stern lesson temporarily impressed on those who employ others in positions of trust. Some people simply refuse to profit from the experience of others. Even the recurring publicity, as the unwelcome spotlight falls on Bangor or Memphis or Topeka, will not shake the complacency of those employers, public and private, who persist in believing that "it won't happen to me!"

If in this book I seem to have taken a harsh and sometimes cynical stance in my observations and advice about embezzlers and embezzlement, it was not with the intention of stimulating harshness or cynicism in those who may read it. One can be, and should be, both idealistic and pragmatic at the same time. The loss of idealism can shrivel the soul, but wishful thinking can never dispel unpleasant realities.

Any employer who would protect himself against employee dishonesty must first face the facts and then take proven steps to reduce his risk. If he fails to act and then suffers loss, he has no one but himself to blame.

There is an old Chinese saying:

May the gods protect me from those I trust.
Against all others I can defend myself.

Such serene faith in celestial intervention may be an Oriental virtue; it is not compatible with the vigorous American tradition of self-reliance.